Emotions, Activism,
and Social Change

Emotions, Activism, and Social Change

DEBORAH J. CANTRELL

Professor of Law

University of Colorado Law School

CAROLINA ACADEMIC PRESS

Durham, North Carolina

Library of Congress Cataloging-in-Publication Data
Names: Cantrell, Deborah J., author.
Title: Emotions, activism, and social change / Deborah J.
    Cantrell.
Description: Durham, North Carolina : Carolina Academic
    Press, LLC, [2024] | Includes bibliographical references
    and index.
Identifiers: LCCN 2024035726 | ISBN 9781531031183
    (paperback) | ISBN 9781531031190 (ebook)
Subjects: LCSH: Activism—Psychological aspects. | Social
    change—Psychological aspects. | Anger—Social aspects.
    | Emotions—Social aspects.
Classification: LCC HM881 .C35 2024 | DDC 303.48/4019
    —dc23/eng/20240904
LC record available at https://lccn.loc.gov/2024035726

CAROLINA ACADEMIC PRESS
700 Kent Street
Durham, North Carolina 27701
(919) 489-7486
www.cap-press.com

Printed in the United States of America

Contents

Introduction

My government makes me angry. The police force makes me angry. Homophobia makes me angry. Luckily, anger is what motivates me. . . . Anger has served me well and we're achieving impact every day.

ZHANAR SEKERBAYEVA, LGBTQ activist[1]

There is a potential untapped power in acknowledging and harnessing women's rightful anger; we have every reason to be angry and it can be channeled very positively into advocacy for ourselves in the workplace, or political and social action, as the recent wave of Women's Marches and feminist campaigns worldwide has shown.

LAURA BATES, feminist writer and activist[2]

Activists believe in anger. Activists believe that anger is motivating, mobilizing, righteous, and productive. Activists also are chided, criticized, and blamed for their anger. Activists use anger to express resistance; while at the same time, they experience anger being used against them as control. In social movement work, anger can feel dichotomous and binary. It either is good or bad. It either is productive or harmful. Our reflexive idea of anger is as a "hot" emotion. In its heat, it gets things done, or it burns people out. What could happen

---

1. Zhanar Sekerbayeva, *My Activism Isn't Motivated By Kindness, It's Motivated By Anger,* AMNESTY INTERNATIONAL, available July 2, 2019, at https://www.amnesty.org/en/latest/impact/2019/07/zhanar-sekerbayeva-from-feminita-on-why-anger-motivates-her-activism/.

2. Will Coldwell, *Anger Is An Energy: How to Turn Fury Into a Force for Good,* THE GUARDIAN, May 13, 2019, available at https://www.theguardian.com/lifeandstyle/2019/may/13/anger-interviews.

if social movement activists interrupted our habits—both actions and thoughts—about anger? If we saw anger with more nuance, how might that impact social movement work? For example, could we make better strategic choices if we distinguished between the kind of anger that seeks revenge from the kind of anger that is intended to call out unjust behavior? Or would it help our social movement communities if we understood, and were attentive to, the ways in which the dominant society has structured rules about anger that reflect gender and racial discrimination? And what might happen if we pay attention to emotions related to social activism other than anger?

This book takes up those questions. It does so not from a place of remove and distance. I am a social activist. I feel and act on emotions in my social change work, including anger. At the same time, I am a legal academic who studies social movements, particularly the lawyers who participate in activist work. In my work, I try and identify ways in which social activists can create a more effective strategy of change, particularly if that strategy includes changing the law. I bring both those selves, with both sets of knowledge, to bear in this book. As such, in some ways, this book may read like a manifesto for social activists articulating a range of benefits that could come from rethinking how emotions get deployed in social movement work. This book also is my effort to put research and theory across several disciplines (sociology, psychology, and law) into closer conversation with each other in order to more fulsomely build out a framework about the role of emotions in social movement work, to consider the ways in which the law is embedded with rules about emotions, and to explore what conditions need to be in place for social activism to succeed at changing the law.

In this book, we will start where activists often start—investigating the ways in which the emotion of anger exists in social movement work and the beliefs about when and why it is critical to effective advocacy. First, we need to understand more generally the construct called "anger." What does it look like? Does it take different forms under different circumstances? Has our understanding of anger changed over time? And how has our understanding of anger changed as that concept has been the subject of research by sociologists, psychologists, and others? Critically, we will consider the ways in which there are sets of rules about who is entitled to express anger and under what conditions. Sociologist Arlie Hochschild has called the work we do to discern those emotion rules and make decisions about whether or not to comply with the rules "emotional labor."[3] As we investigate emotional labor, we will see that the rules change depending on who we are and what communities we belong to. Unsurprisingly, those rules reflect that our society pays attention to who has power and control, and that, in turn, reflects status differences based on race, gender, and other important points of identity. Once we have some foundational knowledge about "anger," we can look more carefully and precisely at that emotion and see that it is not one constant experience across all contexts and across all people. That then lets us investigate the role of anger in social movement work with more precision. We will see that there are several kinds of "anger." There is anger that includes a wish for payback or revenge. There is anger that is intended as a public callout of injustice. There is anger that is intended as a signal to other activists of commitment and loyalty to a cause. There is anger that is an expression of frustration.

Importantly, all kinds of anger share a critical feature—anger is an emotion that exists because people are in relationships among one another. In other words, anger is relational. I am angry because of someone else or because of some group of people. Even when I am angry at myself, I usually feel that way because of something I did (or did not do) to another. For

---

3. *See generally* Arlie Russell Hochschild, *Emotion Work, Feeling Rules, and Social Structure*, 85 AM. J. Soc. 551 (1979) (articulating a theoretical framework for emotional labor through "feeling" and "framing" rules).

example, as an activist, I might get angry at myself because I did not speak up in a group where someone criticized my cause. My anger is relational because it stems from my actions in response to the conduct of others. Understanding that anger is relational is important because it helps us more carefully assess the purpose of anger and the consequences of anger. The question is not just whether I could or should be angry. The question always includes the web of relationships that trigger my anger and that will experience the consequences of my anger. Because social movement work, by definition, involves multiple webs of relationships, we need to be able to accurately assess and describe the many kinds of anger that might be at play. Then we can turn to judging anger.

Judging anger is a task that has been taken up by ancient philosophers, like Aristotle, to contemporary philosophers, like Martha Nussbaum and Amia Srinivasan. Across time, there has been no consensus about whether, when, or how anger is good or bad. Thinkers have put forward reasonable arguments in favor of and opposed to anger. We need to have a working knowledge of those arguments, but we do not need to resolve the disagreements. I will encourage us to see how the disagreements themselves present us with important revelations for social movement work. The first is that anger never exists in the abstract. Anger is always tied to a contextualized goal—I have chosen to express anger because I hope or want something to happen as a result and I think anger is the best way to generate that consequence. For example, as an activist, I might believe that expressing anger is the best way for me to demonstrate to those in power that I will not condone their unjust actions. Or, as an activist, I might believe that the best way for me to show my solidarity with others in my movement is to express my anger. My anger signals to others around me that I am just as committed as they are. The challenge with anger in social activism is that it can carry unhelpful consequences. The consequence of being angry at an injustice can be that I want payback. I may believe that I am made whole only when the wrongdoer suffers for the harm they caused. Or, within my movement community, others may question how loyal and dedicated I am if I do not express my anger at a high enough level.

Social activists, like all people, have to navigate the fact that their expressions of anger can carry both positive and negative consequences. But social activists face a unique challenge because of the expectation that activism must be public. In other words, we expect that social movement work is a kind of resistance that only happens in public. It is ardent. It is intended to be seen and to be disruptive. That commitment to public resistance pushes all of us, activists or not, to expect activists to perform emotional labor that is hot, and reveals the fire in the belly. That commitment has consequences for how all of us perceive the webs of relationship surrounding social movement work. We see "us" and "them,"—no matter what side of the public protest we are on. Our relational lines are rigid and are hardened in the space of public resistance. As a result, I suggest that we forget to pay attention to the ways in which quietude and interior reflection can be important sites for cultivating transformative resistance.

In an effort to dislocate and unsettle our habituated patterns of thinking about social movement work as necessarily requiring a hot version of public resistance, we will consider the work of scholar Kevin Quashie. He has offered a probing cultural contemplation on how quiet and interior reflection can be liberatory and dignity enhancing, especially in light of the expectation that public resistance is *the way* to protest against subordination. Using Quashie's work as a bridge, I then ask us to make an unexpected move—to consider how many faith traditions also have embraced the generative potential of silence and quiet. I make this unexpected move for two reasons. First, the move helps us to become aware of the habit we have in social movement work of seeing webs of relationship only in binary terms—us/them and good/bad. Second, I think that looking at the way faith traditions embrace revelatory knowledge and embrace a sense of connectedness between all living beings helps us to discern a critical dimension of relationality—there is a difference between the *fact* of relationality and the *valence* of relationality. In other words, there is a descriptive fact about relationality, and it is that webs of relationships are a constant descriptive truth in our world. But the valence of relationality—whether any particular web contains positive, negative, or neutral relationships—always is in flux. Not only do different webs of relationships have different valences, but even the same web of relationships can ebb and flow between positive, negative, and neutral. I argue that the possibility that relationships can change presents a critical opportunity for social movement activists. If I can disrupt my habit of only seeing friends or enemies, that opens me to the possibility of finding new and unexpected common ground with others. It also helps me see that I still may need to engage in deeper conversations about differences and disagreements with the people I believe already to be on my side. Importantly, I have to engage in relational work regardless of the current valence of any particular relationship. Having the ability to move into quiet, contemplative, and revelatory mind space improves my chances to foster positive relationships.

It would be sanguine and unhelpful if I did not also chart out concerns and challenges that come with my recommendation that activists rethink the importance that they place on hot anger and public resistance. For example, if it is true that people with power maintain their control in part by vilifying activists (particularly women and people of color) for expressing anger, how do we preserve a way for activists to insist upon their own dignity and power? What does resistance look like if it is not hotly angry? And can we be sure that resistance without hot anger is effective in bringing about social change? The second half of the book turns to those important questions. I begin by considering the counterpart emotion to anger—love. It, too, is an emotion that shows up among activists. Activists speak of their commitments to their cause in love-related terms. We might hear an activist describe how she came to her movement because she loves, or is passionate about, the cause (i.e., "I love the wilderness and I'm passionate about protecting it from development."). Or we hear activists talk about the support and comradery they feel for their movement colleagues, and how important it is to show movement colleagues that they are loved and will be protected.

Just like we did with anger, before we consider whether and how the emotion of love can benefit activists in their work, we first have to more thoroughly understand the concept of "love" and the range of emotional labor rules that relate to it. I explore how the construct of love contains a key expectation about relationality, which is that when we describe a relationship as including love, we assume the relationship is positive. Further, when we focus on emotional labor rules about love and passion in social movement work, we see a similar pattern as with anger. The idea of "love" in social movement work is oppositional—either you are in the movement with me or you are outside of it and against me. To love my social movement colleagues requires me to show a kind of loyalty that is absolute and unyielding. I call that kind of emotional labor "hyper-loyalty." Like anger in social movement work, love also is understood mostly as unidimensional. Love, like anger, in social movement work gets described as the "fire in the belly." As a result, we face a similar conundrum as we did with anger. There are ways in which hyper-loyalty supports and protects activist communities. Hyper-loyalty gives activists comfort that they have a space in which to speak freely with each other without risking censure or opprobrium. At the same time, it overemphasizes differences and too readily embraces antagonism between groups.

But our earlier exploration of more dynamic and fluid experiences of webs of relationships offers us a way to think about how emotional labor could happen in social movement work in ways that are not zero-sum. When we remind ourselves that the fact of relationality is constant, but the valence of relationality regularly changes, that encourages us to expand our understanding of what "love" in social movement work can mean. Importantly, social movement histories themselves give us potent examples. Dr. Martin Luther King, Jr. repeatedly spoke of his belief in a "beloved community" that included all people, and that was created through practices he called "love in action."[4] Dr. King pressed the idea that "love in action" was vigorous and required the calling out of injustice as a means of ensuring that all people had their dignity recognized. As Dr. King conceived of love in social movement work, it was not sentimental and apologetic, but clear-eyed and strong-voiced. It embraced tension and resistance as ways of prompting people to "rise from the bondage of myths and half-truths"[5] that supported racial prejudice and discrimination. Clear-eyed love in action also insisted that the fact of interconnectedness of all people then was the seed from which a beloved community could be created.

More contemporary activist-scholars have offered complementary teachings. Moving from Dr. King's Christian-centered tradition to a Buddhist tradition, I introduce the work of Buddhist theologian, Reverend angel Kyodo williams. Like Dr. King who grounded his work in his faith tradition and Biblical teachings, Reverend williams grounds her work in foundational Buddhist concepts, including a central tenet that all life is interconnected. As a person of color, Reverend

---

4. *See generally* Martin Luther King, Jr., A TESTAMENT OF HOPE: THE ESSENTIAL WRITINGS AND SPEECHES OF MARTIN LUTHER KING, JR. (James Melvin Washington ed., HarperOne 1986).

5. Martin Luther King, Jr., *Letter From Birmingham City Jail*, A TESTAMENT OF HOPE: THE ESSENTIAL WRITINGS AND SPEECHES OF MARTIN LUTHER KING, JR. 291 (James Melvin Washington ed., 1986).

williams also grounds her work in her lived experiences of discrimination, particularly within Buddhist communities in which she has practiced. williams calls her approach "radical dharma"[6]—"dharma" being the Sanskrit word used to refer to the core truths and teachings of Buddhism. Like Dr. King's love in action, the goal of radical dharma is to bring forward the ever-present relationality between all people, and to do so in ways that enhance dignity for everyone and dismantle systems of subordination and oppression. For williams, the method for unearthing that dignity-enhancing relationality is the practice of fierce love. For example, if I am a white person with privilege, fierce love requires me to see how society awards me unearned benefits, to see how my silence and inaction actually support systemic injustice, and to understand that my Buddhist practices for my own liberation are errant if they do not also include my genuine commitment to actions that are just and liberatory for all. If I am a person of color, fierce love supports me in speaking plainly about unjust experiences and in calling forward the range of ways, explicit and tacit, that current members of my community, particularly white members, maintain systems of subordination. At the same time, I do so with the goal of fostering interconnectedness, not dismantling it.

While activism founded on faith traditions is not new—as Dr. King's example illustrates—it is an uncommon frame by which to explore emotional labor in social movement work. Using such a frame may make us pause for a moment, because it is unfamiliar. That is precisely my goal. I encourage us to harness the potential of the unexpected pause. Instead of meeting the unexpected frame with distrust and skepticism, I want us to let the frame create the possibility that we will learn something useful and novel from it. I posit that the clear-eyed and strong-voiced practices of love in action and

---

6. angel Kyodo williams & Rod Owens with Jasmine Syedullah, RADICAL DHARMA: TALKING RACE, LOVE AND LIBERATION (2016).

radical dharma give activists effective ways to call out injustice, but without the payback wish that anger often carries with it. Further, the frame helps us center emotional labor in social movement work around an emotion, love, which is grounded on seeing connections between people and taking actions to maintain and build those connections. Importantly, love in action and fierce love adjust the more common feeling and framing rules about love so that it becomes necessary for each person within a web of relationships to pay attention to the ways in which the web of relationships have unhelpfully adopted unjust and dignity-denying practices.

Once we have created a new foundation for a more positive kind of emotional labor for social movement work, we need to build one more connection before we take up our final inquiry about whether, when, and how anything related to emotional labor matters to activists when their goal is to change the law. That connection is to articulate why and how positive relationality matters to activists other than strengthening relationships within their own groups. Here I again will look to histories within social movement work itself—more particularly, to the history of mutual aid. Mutual aid is the idea that communities can (and should) come together to create services that ensure that community members have their fundamental needs met. For example, if a community has members who face food insecurity, the community can create a no-cost grocery store where folks can come select the foods they need. Or, if a community has members who need no-cost childcare, the community can create a no-cost, neighborhood home-based childcare service. As community members come together in mutual aid, they have opportunities to learn about each other and to learn about ways in which their collective efforts can expand and become more politically active. The Black Panther Party powerfully used mutual aid in the 1960s to catalyze community activism. The Party began providing free meals for school children in Oakland as a way to meet a critical community need, and as a method for bringing community members together and introducing them to the activism of the Party. Legal scholar and activist Dean Spade has written powerfully about the way in which mutual aid catalyzes connection. And, as Spade points out, social change does not happen unless there are enough people supporting and pressing for the change.[7]

The examples of mutual aid help us to see a core fact about social change—we need sufficient numbers of people to make change happen. Thus, we need to be able to build connections between, among, and across movement groups. As activists, we need to be able to see commonality and the possibilities that come with working through difference, instead of focusing on disagreements and fostering distrust. At the same time, working together cannot happen in ways that replicate current systems of injustice or subordination. I think that fierce love provides a set of practices that help activists navigate the dynamism and challenges of interconnectedness.

In the book's final chapter, I take up the question of whether and how emotional labor in social movements is relevant if the change that activists desire is to change the law. As a starting crux move, I illustrate how we often misperceive "the law" as something that is above, or removed from, people. I argue that thinking about the law as disembodied from people creates two key misapprehensions. The first is that we think about "the law" as unmoored from the people who make it. As a result, we may neglect to consider how the law is made by, and for the support of, the people in society who hold power and who wish to maintain power. In other words, "the law" is never neutral. The people who make the law build a certain set of values into the law, and those values often do not seek to benefit all members of society equitably. If we do not remind

---

7. *See* Dean Spade, Mutual Aid: Building Solidarity During This Crisis (and the Next) (2020).

ourselves that "the law" comes from human actions, we may see the law as more neutral than it is, and more removed from people than it is.

Instead, law is deeply relational. Its core responsibility is to organize actions between people who live in communities together. Think of mundane examples, like the law telling me that I have to stop at a red light, because you get to drive at a green light. Or the law telling you that, as an employer, you cannot fire me, your employee, just because I am getting older. We often experience the law in the binary—either the law is in your favor, or it is in your opponent's favor. I argue that the dominant perception of the law as about individual winners or losers subtly assists those with power to hold on to power. The law gets enforced by creating adversaries, not allies. If I want to get a benefit from the law, I have to sue you. I do not generally get to sue the people who made the law on the grounds that they made an unjust law.

We can change that dynamic by seeing law's relationality in its fullest, especially in those settings where the more obvious relationality is binary and adversarial. I use the law of personal injury (called tort law) as an example, where one person sues another for a harm caused by the other's bad conduct. More particularly, I look at how tort law has developed in a way that subtly privileges paying back the more powerful people in society for harms they suffer. Using the work of legal scholars Martha Chamallas and Scott Skinner-Thompson, we will see how men have benefitted from the way tort law calculates their lost wages compared to women, and how straight people have benefitted in harms related to invasions of privacy compared with LGBTQ people. When we unearth the more subtle ways that the law controls much larger webs of relationality, I argue that we also unearth the possibility of bringing more people together in an effort to create change. If changing the law requires bringing the greatest number of people into the effort, then finding common ground helps that endeavor.

The second key misapprehension that happens when we disembody the law is that we can mistakenly imbue "the law" with some special capacity to make change on its own. We mistakenly think that changing the law necessarily will lead to changing every person's view. In other words, we think the law has some special forcefulness to drive change. If we take a moment to think about the history of laws designed to end segregation, I think we readily see that the law *does not* have special power to change minds. By keeping the law tethered to the people who make it, we, as activists, have to confront the question of what other work we need to do to support people changing their minds. I look at the history of activism related to marriage equality to see how that dynamic can unfold. Author and journalist Sasha Issenberg has chronicled the roughly quarter-century of activism that ultimately led to both federal and state laws recognizing marriage as a legal union available to a couple regardless of sex or gender identity. As Issenberg documents, early activist efforts in the 1960s were led by lesbian feminists who were critical of marriage as an institution, and whose efforts focused on expanding the legal definition of family so that it would include LGBTQ couples—particularly gay or lesbian parents who wanted to maintain relationships with children they had from straight marriages.[8] But, the conservative response to those efforts was framed in a more focused way and centered on preserving marriage as available only between one man and one woman. That focus shifted the LGBTQ activist strategy because it appeared that the way to garner more people in support of a range of outcomes that enhanced the lives of LGBTQ people was not to accept the focus on marriage as an institution, but to push people to think about marriage equality as necessary for human dignity for all. That framing brought along most

---

8. *See* Sasha Issenberg, THE ENGAGEMENT: AMERICA'S QUARTER-CENTURY STRUGGLE OVER SAME-SEX MARRIAGE (2022).

LGBTQ people and brought in straight allies. The coalition grew because members saw how their lives—with their joys and struggles—were similar to each other.

I think a key feature of all of my examples about the law is that in organizing relationships, the law also creates rules about expected emotional labor. For example, in tort law, the law creates a wrongdoer and a victim who is harmed. If I am the person who has been harmed, the law says that I am entitled to be angry and to seek payback from the wrongdoer. Similarly, historically, family law has said that certain legal rights attach only to certain relationships. It also has set up expectations about the emotional labor that is supposed to happen within those relationships—what kinds of actions constitute "love," who is supposed to show what feelings to whom, and the like.

Because the law is deeply relational, it prescribes and orchestrates emotional labor. Thus, all of the discoveries we have made earlier in the book about emotional labor in social movement work need to be brought to bear when we, as activists, think that we need to change the law. We need to be able to see the ways in which our current expectations about emotional labor in activism help us catalyze and grow webs of relationships, and when our emotional labor discourages relationality. In turn, we need to be able to cultivate some equanimity about the fact that anger in social movement work is complicated. It can be good and bad at the very same time. It can enhance dignity and degrade dignity at the very same time. It can be used to resist and to control at the very same time. Because anger in social movement work is complicated, it may be less effective at helping us achieve social change than we would hope. Let us explore those inquiries together more thoroughly in the coming chapters.

Emotions, Activism, and Social Change

1

Describing Anger

WHEN I SAY TO FOLKS who are engaged in social movements that anger is the predominant emotion expressed by social activists, they typically respond by nodding their heads "yes" and replying that people *should be* angry about the injustice that the activist is working to remedy. Activists expect that they will feel and show anger as they do their work. In other words, it is *descriptively* true and accurate that a primary set of sensations that activists experience when they do their work is called "anger." Further, activists believe that anger is the correct emotion for them to express as a way of showing the value that they place on their work and on the outcome of their activism. In other words, it is *normatively* true and accurate for activists to feel and express anger at the current state of affairs in their community. When we stop and take a moment to think about the concept of "anger," I think we quickly see that "anger" has several incarnations. Different situations can prompt us to express anger in different ways. If we want to understand and assess the role of anger in helping an activist produce social change, we first need to understand the nuances between the types of expressions that all get labeled "anger." This chapter takes up that more thorough-going descriptive exploration of anger. It lays the foundation for the follow-on normative inquiry in the next chapter about how we judge the efficacy of anger.

This chapter takes as a starting point the wellspring of existing research that has found that anger is a dominant emotion for social activists.[1] That research is backed up by a ready supply of ordinary examples that I think all activists can come up with about the anger they have experienced in their own work. Thus, I do not think it is unexpected or radical to describe social activism as including anger as a dominant emotion. Therefore, what we need to investigate is what *kinds* of anger predominate in movement work. I do want to note that while our focus will be on anger, it is not the only emotion that social activists experience. Research shows that anger often can be joined by other emotions such as loyalty, fear, platonic love, and shame.[2] But anger is a key catalyzing emotion for social activism. As we will see, it also can have complicated consequences that create challenges for activists. It will be helpful to start by laying some general groundwork that will help us categorize anger. Then, we will focus more specifically on anger in social movement work.

When we think generally about anger, we think about it as one of the emotions that people feel and express when they are upset or unhappy about something. For example, there is a kind of anger that is quick and reactive like when I shout out if someone cuts me off while I am driving. There is the kind of anger that stems from a personal wrong or grudge, like when I avoid a family member because they said or did

---

1. See Helena Flam, *Emotions' Map*, in EMOTIONS AND SOCIAL MOVEMENTS 19–22 (Helena Flam & Debra King eds., 2005); James M. Jasper, *Constructing Indignation: Anger Dynamics in Protest Movements*, 6 EMOTION REV. 208 (2014).

2. *See* James M. Jasper, *Emotions and Social Movements: Twenty Years of Theory and Research*, 37 ANN. REV. SOC. 285 (2011).

something I found personally hurtful. There also is a kind of anger that is seated in some broader social and moral context. That kind of anger often is focused on larger wrongs. For example, if I perceive an injustice in a social policy or larger societal system, I use anger to express my sense of injustice. I expect that each of my examples of anger feels familiar. However, what we may not have paid much attention to is the fact that we use one label, anger, to capture a wide range of actions. When the car driver cuts me off, I might display my anger with a quick shout. When I am angry with my family member who derided me, I might express my anger without words at all, and without directly confronting the family member. When I am angry about a social injustice, it may become important to me to show my anger very publicly, including becoming part of a social movement.

When we take some time to break apart the idea of "anger," it helps us see that there actually are multiple constructions of anger. By breaking apart the idea of anger, we also start to see that different constructions about anger carry sets of rules with them about when anger is an acceptable response, and who is permitted to use it. Further, how I express anger is not just about me and how I want to feel. Oftentimes, my expression of anger is more about my desire to communicate a message to others. I want you to know that I am angry because I want *you* to change your behavior in some way.

That said, a person's expression of anger can also be situated in a broader set of relationships and a broader set of social rules and regulations. As we think particularly about the role of anger for social activists, we need to pay attention to the rules about emotions in relationships between individuals as well as the rules about emotions among societal groups. As we will see, activists have a set of expectations and rules about the role of anger in their work. Those expectations often can be very different than the rules that the dominant group in society has about who is entitled to express anger. Therefore, if we want to more clearly assess the role anger *does* play in social activism, and the role it *should* play, we first need to have a more robust understanding about several features of anger. For example, we need to know whether research confirms that some part of the brain triggers some standard set of physical reactions that we understand as anger. Finally, we need to understand how cognition constructs social concepts. In other words, how do we learn the rules related to emotions like anger? It will help us if we have a fuller and more nuanced description of anger before we turn to judging when and how it helps social activists reach their goals. We will turn to judging anger in the next chapter.

Picking up from the quick examples about anger above, let us start first by better understanding how anger can be expressed.

Differing Expressions of Anger

One conception of anger is the kind of quick, reactive response that feels almost instinctual. It is the kind of expression that we might exhibit if someone unexpectedly shoves us hard from behind, startling us, and prompting us to turn around and yell out, "Hey, stop that!" We generally think of this kind of anger as being connected to evolution and to behaviors that were adapted in order to keep us physically safe. We believe that this kind of reflexive anger arises quickly when triggered and may be harder to control. When we get unexpectedly shoved, we yell out before we have time to take in more information—information which might let us know that the person who shoved us was not trying to harm us at all. That person might have been knocked into us by another, or might have been trying to move out of the way of an oncoming vehicle, or some other action that we would have taken ourselves. But our reflex to protect ourselves can trigger that "fight" response that we label anger.

We also describe anger as a set of feelings that arise when we experience some kind of hurtful treatment. The hurtful action might be small, as when a child gets angry when her sibling takes away a favorite toy. Or the action might be more serious, as when a colleague speaks callously and dismissively about us. This kind of anger typically involves one person treating another person in a hurtful way. We often expect that it can lead to the harmed person holding a grudge or desiring to get back at the person who instigated the harm. We generally think of this kind of anger as arising after some assessment of the other's conduct. While we might experience some quick sensations at the time of the other's behavior, we usually cogitate on the conduct before concluding that the other person has wronged us. Further, if we conclude that we are angry, we generally justify our anger using moral language. For example, we might justify being angry at our work colleague by saying that a workplace can only be effective if all workers treat each other with respect and civility. Or we might describe the colleague's actions as violating the "Golden Rule" of "do unto others as you would have them do unto you." Further, we justify holding a grudge because we believe the other person has violated some kind of shared social compact and should be held accountable for that breach. But the breach typically relates to individuals and conduct between them. This kind of anger reflects a range of socially constructed beliefs and behaviors. It contrasts with reflexive anger, which focuses on the body's "freeze, fight, flight" responses. Importantly, because this kind of anger is socially constructed, that creates room for us to agree and disagree with each other about whether any particular set of circumstances, in fact, justify the way that an individual feels and expresses anger.

Finally, there is the form anger takes when we mean it to show our moral outrage at a larger, more systemic kind of harm. For example, when a group experiences unfair and unjust systemic discrimination, and members say they are angry, they usually mean more than that they are upset and harmed by another individual's actions towards them. They also mean that they are upset and harmed by a larger societal system that causes collective, morally wrong outcomes. A ready example is anger over racially discriminatory outcomes for people of color who are sent through the U.S. criminal justice system. Often, when someone says they are angry and that they mean their anger to call out a systemic injustice, the desired way forward is to change the system for the better of all. In other words, the desired outcome of anger-as-injustice is forward-looking. In contrast, when anger is more a response to the bad behavior of a specific person, the desired outcome is individually focused. The harmed person hopes that that bad-acting person gets payback for the bad conduct.

Of course, my distinctions between kinds of anger make it seem like there are clearer lines than there are. I can be angry at an individual who harms me because that individual is acting in ways that demonstrate a systemic injustice. I might want that individual to have to account for their bad behavior *and* want to change a systemic injustice so that things are better for everyone going forward. While acknowledging that the lines between types of anger are blurry, I want to map out some archetypes about social activists and the three expressions of anger described above. I think my examples will help us see that anger is not something that just exists on its own. It always and ineluctably is socially constructed. Nonetheless, it will be important to remind ourselves that the archetypes below are simplified and necessarily miss important nuances.

The Angry Mob: In early sociological work investigating social activism, researchers started with the idea that anger could coalesce a group into a protesting mob that would be unruly and could easily behave violently.[3] People within the mob responded to each other's anger in an escalating fashion and the

---

3. Gustave Le Bon, THE CROWD: A STUDY OF THE POPULAR MIND (1895).

"mob" took on a life of its own. It was as if anger was a virus that was transmitted from person to person. Once infected, a person had little ability to control their behavior. Anger under mob theory always produced behavior that was unruly, disruptive, disrespectful, and potentially dangerous to others and to property. Mob theory's anger was reflexive, infectious to others, labeled "irrational," and typically considered immoral.

The Stalwart Protestor: Another view of anger in social activism is that it is the wellspring that keeps a social activist going in her work. Think of the common phrase I used earlier about an activist having the "fire in the belly" that motivates her work. The behaviors that are associated with this stalwart conception of anger can include disruptive behavior, like a protest march that stops traffic, but, unlike the angry mob, the disruptive behavior maintains some control. Protestors keep marching and ignore others who scream at them. Protestors stand steady when they meet a line of police in riot gear. Further, stalwart anger often is described by protestors as a way of insisting on dignity and respect. For example, in the 1970s, women organized "Take Back the Night" marches in order to protest against sexual violence. The marches were designed to reclaim nighttime as a safe time for women to be out in public without fearing for their safety. Women marched, sang, or chanted, and often carried candles or signs. They called on men to treat them with equal respect and dignity. This kind of anger often is understood as rational and under a person's control.

The Defiant Activist: Yet another view of anger in social activism is that it is an appropriate and important way to defy subordination. For those activists working in places or on issues where they are trying to reclaim power that has been unjustly used to control them, anger is a way to publicly show that they intend to defy that unjust control. Think about some of the early protests during the AIDS pandemic in the 1980s by the group, ACT UP. The group's acronym stood for "AIDS

Coalition to Unleash Power," and its motto included that its members were "united in anger . . . to end the AIDS crisis." ACT UP used anger as a signal of defiance against the mainstream healthcare system and its unwillingness to prioritize work on a disease that initially impacted marginalized people, like gay men. More recently, activists working within the Black Lives Matter movement also have used anger as a way of signaling their defiance towards policies that have unjust consequences for people of color and that were enacted by predominantly white politicians. This kind of anger often gets understood in dichotomous ways. For the activists, their anger rationally stems from their unjust subordination and by clearly expressing their anger they are being forthright in expressing their sense of injustice. For opponents, defiant anger is a very small step away from the irrational anger of an unruly mob. Thus, opponents decry defiant anger as unhelpful and distracting.

When we map the three different kinds of anger onto the three archetypes of social activism, I think we see some interesting patterns. First, we can see some obvious similarities between the idea of reactive, instinctual anger and the idea of social activists as an angry mob. Both views are grounded in a more classical view of emotions as different than and separate from the "thinking" part of the brain. Further, under the classical view, the thinking part of the brain is rational whereas emotions are irrational. Thus, anger, even if it might have had an original, evolutionary purpose of alerting to danger, now has settled into a reflexive, irrational response. The collective version of such a reflexive, irrational response is the angry mob. Under the classical view of social activism, group members' actions trigger each other's reflexive responses, almost as if an emotion like anger is an infectious disease. The irrational emotion then causes irrational behavior like mob violence. Researchers have discovered that only a few features of the classical view of emotions are accurate, such as the fact that there are some ways in which emotions can be experienced quickly and reflexively.[4] However, research on both emotions generally, and emotions and social activism more particularly, show that the story is more complicated—and more interesting.

Over the last decade, neuroscientists and psychologists have better refined their understanding of emotions, especially as brain-imaging technology has improved. Brain imaging has allowed researchers to map what parts of the brain are activated and in use when a person reports that they are experiencing an emotion. Under the classical theory of emotions, researchers hypothesized that when certain areas of the brain showed activity, that then would result in a person displaying some behaviors associated with an emotion. For example, researchers concluded from early imaging studies that when the amygdala region of the brain was active, that meant someone was experiencing fear, and thus would display some behavior related to fear—freezing, fleeing, or fighting.[5] Researchers initially concluded that the amygdala was the part of the brain that triggered a set of reflexive responses related to fear, and that other parts of the brain could intercede and regulate (or rationalize) those reflexive responses. But, as additional studies were conducted, the data showed that the amygdala was activated across a range of reported emotions, including being happy or sad.[6] Further, no matter the emotion, many other regions of the brain are active as well.[7]

There is little empirical support that any particular part of the brain triggers particular behaviors that are associated with displaying a specific emotion. In other words, there are

---

4. *See, e.g.,* James M. Jasper, *supra* note 2.

5. *See* Maria Gendron, *The Evolving Neuroscience of Emotion: Challenges and Opportunities for Integration with the Law*, *in* Research Handbook on Law and Emotion 27 (Susan A. Bandes et al. eds., 2021).

6. *Id.* at 29.

7. *Id.* at 29–30.

not parts of the brain that *cause* emotions. Instead, current theories posit that there are networks of brain activity that are involved whenever we have to process information—either because we are experiencing some set of bodily sensations, or recalling a memory, or hearing new information.[8] No matter how we articulate what we are doing—whether by saying we are experiencing an emotional state or saying we are "thinking"—the networks in our brains get activated. Thinking and feeling both are mental activities. Further, current neuroscience theories acknowledge that the idea of emotions is, itself, constructed. In other words, we learn from the community that surrounds us what counts as an "emotion"—it is a socially constructed idea and not something innate and existing on its own. The constructed concept of "emotion" includes information about the physical sensations occurring in our bodies, the settings in which that occurs, and how others around us are reacting or responding. Our brain networks contain that socially constructed learning, and our brains use that information when processing some experience or stimuli.[9] The result of our information processing is our assessment that we are angry, or sad, or happy, or disappointed, and the like.

Social scientists studying group activism have had a similar trajectory to neuroscientists and cognitive psychologists. The mob theory of social activism that arose in the 19th century was based on the classical idea of an emotion as being different from cognition. A mob of people could trigger in each other reflexive emotions, like anger or fear, that then triggered reflexive behaviors that were outside the control of the cognitive, rational part of the brain. Mobs were presumed to be unruly and potentially dangerous because of those reflexive, irrational emotions. But as social scientists started to more rigorously study social activists and to collect data on

---

8. *Id.* at 31–35.
9. *Id.*

what factors actually motivated activism, the mob theory was quickly replaced.

Instead, researchers began to focus on other features, like resources that activists reported were critical for their work to succeed. Those resources could include tangible things such as access to safe meeting spaces for groups of people, or money, as well as more intangible items like access to sympathetic politicians or other policymakers. Resource mobilization theory foregrounded a wide range of behaviors that showed how activists thought out their work, and created strategies to make their activism effective.[10] In other words, activists were not motivated by seemingly unruly emotions unbounded by thinking and planning. In some ways, resource mobilization theories portrayed activists as hyper-rational. Activists assessed the range of resources available to them, did a cost-benefit analysis, and then crafted a strategy in light of that analysis.

That overly rational approach opened resource mobilization theories to criticism that the theories ignored the emotional dimension that comes with all human activities, including social activism. Current theories of social activism have adjusted for that omission and explicitly consider the ways in which emotions inform and support how social activists are motivated to engage in their work, and how they frame and construct their activism.[11] Like neuroscience theories of constructed networks in the brain, social sciences theorize that culture plays a crucial role in how people construct emotions—what emotions look like, how they feel, what they mean, and when and how emotions are displayed. Those cultural theories recognize that social activists have learned and

---

10. *See* John D. McCarthy and Mayer N. Zald, *Resource Mobilization and Social Movements: A Partial Theory*, 82 AM. J. SOC. 1212 (1977); *see also* J. Craig Jenkins, *Resource Mobilization Theory and the Study of Social Movements*, 9 ANN. REV. SOC. 527 (1983).

11. *See generally* EMOTIONS AND SOCIAL MOVEMENTS (Helena Flam et al. eds., 2005).

experienced what it means to be angry or joyful or to identify some action as unjust. Activists learn what kinds of behaviors they (and others) are expected to perform in order to show the emotions that are relevant to their activist work. Thus, researchers consider not only what resources a group may have available in order to make its work successful, but also that range of social constructions about emotions that the group takes up in its work, and whether and when those emotions are useful to the work.[12]

The examples of the stalwart protestor and the defiant protestor nicely represent the move in both neurosciences and social sciences to treat emotions and thinking as integrated and dynamic processes within the brain that develop over time through experience and learning. For example, being a stalwart protestor can reflect a very intentional, strategic choice to display emotions in ways that preclude others from dismissing the protestor as angry and irrational. In that way, the stalwart protestor hopes to pressure others to engage with her substantive message and to take away others' ability to dismiss her activism as unthoughtful. The stalwart protestor knows through learning or experience about tropes like the angry mob, and uses that same learning and experience to craft a set of choices about what kinds of emotions she will display and for what purposes.

The defiant protestor engages the same cognitive processes and cognitive networks of learning and experience, but she makes a different strategic choice. The defiant protestor intends to meet head-on the conventional trope of the unruly, irrational protestor and to insist instead that to be angry and loud about an injustice is to act rationally. The defiant protes-

---

12. *See* Ron Eyerman, *How Social Movements Move, in* EMOTIONS AND SOCIAL MOVEMENTS, *supra* note 5 at 41; *see also* Francesca Polletta and James Jasper, *Collective Identity and Social Movements*, 27 ANN. REV SOC. 283 (2001); Robert D. Benford and David A. Snow, *Framing Processes and Social Movements: An Overview and Assessment*, 26 ANN. REV. SOC. 611 (2000).

tor likely also intends to challenge a range of social constructions related to emotions that reflect bias—along gender, race, and class. I will return to biasing in emotions in more detail shortly.

The examples of the stalwart protestor and the defiant protestor also give us an opportunity to consider the relational dynamic present not only in social activism, but in all expressions of emotions. Sociologist Arlie Hochschild developed the concept of emotional labor to capture a range of cognitive and expressive processes that a person undertakes when making choices about how to express an emotion.[13] Further, the emotional labor that a person undertakes is not a solitary activity. It reflects a web of relationships the person sits within and her assessments of how her choices will impact others and what their reactions might be. Hochschild begins with the cultural rules we learn about what emotions we are supposed to feel in any given situation. She calls those "feeling" rules.[14] For example, we may have grown up in a web of relationships where we learned a feeling rule that we are supposed to feel happy when it is our birthday. A feeling rule also comes along with a set of embodied behaviors that we act out to demonstrate the feeling. For example, we demonstrate that we are happy on our birthday by smiling and laughing when we receive birthday wishes or gifts. As I noted, feeling rules are culturally constructed and are not universal. We could have grown up in a web of relationships where the feeling rule about birthdays was that we are to be somber and contemplative because birthdays are a moment to reflect back on one's life. We might express that feeling rule by being quiet and reserved when receiving a birthday wish.

---

13. *See generally* Arlie Russell Hochschild, *Emotion Work, Feeling Rules, and Social Structure*, 85 Am. J. Soc. 551 (1979).

14. *Id.* at 563–66.

A feeling rule engages with our cognitive networks that contain learned information and experiences about an emotion. A feeling rule helps us both choose an emotion to display and to make choices about how to use our body—to change facial expressions or to disrupt a reflexive feeling and replace it with some other action. For example, if we have learned a feeling rule about being happy on our birthday, and we find ourselves frowning or showing some other signs of a negative emotion, we may remind ourselves to change our physical behaviors to comport with the "happy" feeling rule. Importantly, feeling rules are not reflexive. In any particular situation, we must make a choice about what feeling rule applies as well as whether we want to comport with the feeling rule that we have learned. Consider the defiant protestor again. She knows that there are certain feeling rules that say that the acceptable way to protest is to be calm and collected. The defiant protestor considers that the feeling rule has been socially constructed, at least in part, by those in her community with power who wish to maintain control. By refusing to comply with the feeling rule, the defiant protestor intends to reject a rule that she believes is designed to constrain what she experiences as a legitimate and just grievance.

In addition to feeling rules, Hochschild describes framing rules.[15] Framing rules are ideological rules that ascribe meanings to situations. A feeling rule tells us how to feel and a framing rule tells us why. To take the birthday example again, if our feeling rule is that we are to be happy on birthdays, the related framing rule is that birthdays are moments where people who love us come together to celebrate and uplift us. Being celebrated and uplifted are positive and supportive actions towards us, and, thus, warrant us feeling happy. Of course, since framing rules also are socially constructed, there can be more than one framing rule for a situation and people can

---

15. *Id.* at 566–68.

disagree about which framing rule is most appropriate. The stalwart protestor and the defiant protestor express different emotions in protest in part because they use different framing rules about the meaning they ascribe to protest.

Emotional labor is the overall endeavor required by feeling rules and framing rules given the setting or situation. I perform emotional labor when I assess that a particular setting requires me to be happy, and that means that I should make myself smile. When we speak about emotions, we often talk as if our emotional labor is just about the internal goings-on in our head and our bodies. I say that I am happy or sad or I ask you if you are happy or sad. It is as if emotions are solely created and contained within each of us individually. But the idea of emotional labor inherently calls on us to be aware of others around us. In almost all settings, we think about and experience emotions in the context of a web of relationships. Thus, our emotional labor is not a solitary endeavor. Instead it is deeply relational.

It is relational in a micro sense in that we consider the specific individuals around us to whom we wish to signal some intent about our emotion, or whom we wish to influence with our display of emotion, or to whom we are responding because of their conduct. Emotional labor is relational in a macro sense in that it considers a range of meanings that reflect cultural or societal values reflected within the web of relationships that make up the social structure around us. Thus, when we are performing emotional labor, we often have to navigate different kinds of relationality. I may have to consider both how the person I know really well is going to respond and how outside observers whom I do not know well are going to respond.

By its very nature, social activism requires participants constantly to pay attention to relationality. Activists have to toggle back and forth between micro-level and macro-level emotional labor. When an activist is in a small group meeting with her activist peers, she engages in emotional labor that most likely foregrounds features about the personal relationships she has with those peers. For example, if she is new to the group, she may feel pressure to show her peers that she is genuinely committed to the cause. So, the new activist engages in emotional labor that her peers will read as commitment. That might include behaviors like clapping loudly when a peer speaks, adding vehemence to her voice when the activist talks, or making denigrating statements about opponents of the group. When the activist moves to larger settings where personal relationships are not the focus, the activist likely focuses on her role as part of her activist group. Her emotional labor relates to choices the group has made about how it, as a group, wants to display its emotions. The audience for the emotional labor is external to the group, and may be broad and varied. The group's choices may or may not be similar to the choices the activist has made for herself internally within the group.

Further, there may be differences between settings in what framing rules apply to the same behaviors. In the small group setting, speaking with vehemence is framed positively as a way to demonstrate commitment, whereas in a large setting that same behavior may be framed negatively as disrespectful and inappropriate. In all of those moments, the activist is not just thinking about herself and what emotions she is choosing for her own internal reasons. She is thinking about what her co-activists expect from her, as well as performing the emotional labor needed to show cohesion within a group, as well as discerning the dynamics related to a range of external audiences and their expectations. In both micro and macro moments of emotional labor, the activist has to assess what feeling and framing rules might apply not only to her, but to her as part of an activist group, and to her as a member of a broader community. She then has to navigate all of those levels of relationality when she decides whether to comport with the range of feeling rules.

Understanding the relationality of emotional labor enables us to see some important features about socially constructed emotions. The first is one already noted above—the same emotion can have multiple expressions. The fact that anger is not displayed or understood in only one way reflects differences across webs of relationships. I am supposed to feel and display anger one way if I am a parent interacting with my child. I am supposed to feel and display anger differently when I am waiting at a bus stop and someone rudely shoves the elderly person standing next to me. In other words, feeling and framing rules create expectations about when and how we are to express a particular version of an emotion and those feeling and framing rules pay attention to what set of relationships are in play. Importantly, feeling and framing rules vary not only because webs of relationships vary, but also because we can disagree about the norms that animate the rules. The next section looks at some of those disagreements, in particular, disagreements related to when, to whom, and how anger may be expressed.

Differing Norms About Who Gets to Be Angry

Like many emotions, anger has feeling and framing rules that reflect biases—about gender, about race, and about class, among others. Let us consider gender and race in more detail.

Feminist activists and scholars have richly detailed the ways in which anger has been constructed by patriarchal society so that men maintain control over women.[16] One form

---

16. *See* Audre Lorde, *The Uses of Anger*, 9 Women's Stud. Q. 6 (1981); Marilyn Frye, *A Note On Anger*, *in* The Politics of Reality: Essays in Feminist Theory 84 (1893); Sonya Chemaly, Rage Becomes Her: The Power of Women's Anger (2018); Brittney Cooper, Eloquent Rage: A Black Feminist Discovers Her Superpower (2018); Rebecca Traister, Good

of control can be seen in feeling and framing rules that instruct women that they are not to display anger. Some rules are direct—think about the phrase, "It is impolite for women to show anger." Some rules are indirect—think about rules that are supposedly complimentary—"Women are natural caregivers and know how to express their love." That indirect rule, however, is intended to convey that to be a good caregiver means a woman is to express love and not anger.

The rules generally presume that a woman can make choices about what emotions to display. The rules are designed to apply across the enormous range of settings in which women make choices about how to react and what behaviors to display. Further, the rules are designed to constrict women's choices. One key reason is that those who hold power and wish to retain it (men) understand that emotions are used to signal norms and values. One set of values that anger is used to signal relate to disagreement, unfairness, or injustice. But gender-biased feeling and framing rules instruct women that while men may display anger to show that they disagree or have been treated unfairly or unjustly, women may not. Gender-biased feeling and framing rules are designed to disempower women by keeping them quiet about their subordination. Or biased rules are used to shame women if they act out of step with the rules. A woman who expresses her anger at being treated unfairly is dismissed as "irrational" or "hysterical." In contrast, a man who speaks out and expresses anger at being treated unfairly is applauded for having courage and "a backbone." We can readily call to mind a host of everyday phrases that reflect gendered feeling and framing rules about anger. A woman is a shrew if she expresses anger. Women are told to "calm down" when they speak up in ways

AND MAD: THE REVOLUTIONARY POWER OF WOMEN'S ANGER (2018); Alice A. Keefe, *Tending the Fire of Anger*, 39 BUDDHIST-CHRISTIAN STUD. 67 (2019).

that demonstrate anger. Women are told they should smile more often. All of those phrases instruct women that the kind of emotional labor they are expected to perform related to anger requires them to acquiesce to the status quo.

Feeling and framing rules about anger also are racially biased in ways designed to maintain control or dismiss the views and experiences of people of color.[17] Racially biased rules teach that a person of color who expresses anger is being irrational. Further, racially biased rules about anger add conceptions of risk and fear—white people should be afraid when a person of color is angry because the person of color will act out and become violent. Racially biased rules reincorporate the old, inaccurate conception of anger as necessarily leading to violent behavior once triggered. Like gender-biased rules, we can readily call to mind a host of everyday phrases that reflect racial bias. The Black man or Black woman who gets dismissed as the "Angry Black Man/Woman" when the same actions taken by a white person would not draw a comment at all. People of color, especially Black people, getting dismissed as "uppity." Like dismissals of women who express anger, dismissals of people of color are designed to maintain power and control.

Further, people in the socially dominant group are taught biased-feeling rules as if those rules are neutral. For example, research shows that white people looking at facial expressions of a Black person are more ready to identify that person as angry than when looking at similar expressions on a white

---

17. Audrey Lorde, *The Uses of Anger*, *supra* note 16; Mia McKenzie, *Am I a Bully? One Angry Black Woman's Reflection*, in Black Girl Dangerous: On Race, Queerness, Class and Gender 129 (2014); Brittney Cooper, Eloquent Rage: A Black Feminist Discovers Her Superpower, *supra* note 16; Myisha Cherry, The Case for Rage: Why Anger Is Essential to Anti-Racist Struggle (2021).

face.[18] A white person is not intending to misread the facial expressions of a Black person. The white person likely would report that she would interpret facial expressions in the same way no matter who was displaying those expressions. But the white person misreads facial expressions because she is processing that information through racially biased rules, often without consciously understanding that feeling rules can be biased.

One result of biased feeling and framing rules is that there are disparities in the kinds of emotional labor that subordinated groups undertake compared to the dominant group. The rules that apply to a member of the dominant group typically give the person more leeway. For example, when a white man is deciding how to respond to someone who treats him unfairly, the white man knows he has a range of choices, including displaying anger. While he needs to consider the web of relationships involved in the situation as he decides how to respond, he typically can prioritize his own personal interests without much risk of negative consequences. In contrast, a woman of color has more burdensome and more complicated emotional labor. She has to decide what the costs to herself are of complying with biased feeling and framing rules when those rules limit her range of responses. She has to assess the costs of refusing to comply with biased feeling and framing rules in order to be able to express an emotion that is valid for others to express in the same situation. She has to assess the costs not only to herself, but also to other women and people of color around her who may experience collateral consequences (i.e., "We tried putting a woman in that role in the company, but she got angry. That role is better filled by someone who can keep their emotions under control.")

---

18. Joshua M. Ackerman et al., *They All Look the Same to Me (Unless They're Angry): From Out-Group Homogeneity to Out-Group Heterogeneity*, 17 Psychol. Sci. 836 (2006); Amy G. Halberstadt et al., *Preservice Teachers' Racialized Emotion Recognition, Anger Bias, and Hostility Attributions*, 54 Contemp. Edu. Psychol. 125 (2018).

Consider now how biased feeling and framing rules impact how we understand emotions and social activism. To start, biased rules related to emotional labor have, themselves, become flash points for activism. Biased rules related to anger have been particularly called out because those rules get experienced directly as unjust power and control. A key emotional labor rule about anger is that it is the correct emotion to display when we want to express disapproval about an injustice. To say angrily to someone, "Don't do that," is to not only ask the person to stop some behavior, but to signal to that person (and others observing) that the conduct was morally unacceptable. When an emotional labor rule is constructed so that certain groups of people are not permitted to express anger, the point of the restricted rule is to keep those groups under control—either by silencing entirely or by notably limiting potentially disruptive speech or actions.

By definition, social activism involves speaking out. Thus, it makes sense for activists to take on a rule that is intended to silence. Black, feminist writer/poet/activist Audre Lorde has written extensively and eloquently about the necessity and justness of anger in the lives of women, and particularly women of color. As she has said:

> Every woman has a well-stocked arsenal of anger potentially useful against those oppressions, personal and institutional, which brought that anger into being. Focused with precision it can become a powerful source of energy serving progress and change. . . . [A]nger expressed and translated into action in the service of our vision and future is a liberating and strengthening act of clarification. . . . Anger is loaded with information and energy.[19]

Lorde's quote precisely illustrates some features about anger in social activism that can make it more dynamic and

---

19. Audre Lorde, *The Uses of Anger*, *supra* note 16 at 8.

complicated than the kinds of anger that show up in more prosaic settings. The anger expressed by a social activist is notably different than the anger the young child expressed when her sibling took away her favorite toy. When a social activist publicly displays anger, she intends that emotion to signal that she is calling out a moral wrong. She also often intends her anger to be received as overtly defying biased feeling and framing rules. Because emotional labor always is relational, though, the social activist still must anticipate and consider a range of responses by others to her choices about using anger. And we need to remember that an activist's emotional labor is not limited to public settings. The activist also performs emotional labor when making choices about anger within her movement and among other advocates.

In this chapter, I have offered a more fulsome description of anger and the ways in which it is socially constructed. As part of describing anger, I have noted some settings in which there are contradictory feeling and framing rules about anger. We judge anger as both normatively good and normatively bad. And the same setting can prompt one group of people to judge anger as a good and just response, while another group of people in the same setting judge anger as bad and unjust. In order to more clearly assess anger's role in producing effective social activism, it will be helpful to more thoroughly understand the arguments used to judge anger. The next chapter takes up that inquiry.

2

Judging Anger

THERE IS A LONGSTANDING DEBATE among moral and political philosophers about whether anger is good or bad—for individuals and their own wellbeing, and for societies more generally. In order to understand and judge the role of anger in social activism, it will be helpful to understand the broader debate about anger. After laying out that broader debate, the chapter will investigate whether we are able to conclude anything useful about whether anger is good or bad for social activists individually and for social movements collectively.

Philosopher Agnes Callard describes the debate about anger as having two camps. The pro-anger camp "conceive[s] of anger—up to a point—as an essential and valuable part of [a person's] repertoire: anger is what sensitizes us to injustice and motivates us to uphold justice."[1] The anti-anger camp thinks "that we would have a morally better world if we would

---

1. Agnes Callard, *On Anger*, in ON ANGER 13 (Deborah Chasman & Joshua Cohen eds., 2020).

eradicate anger entirely" because it necessarily is, or becomes, "vengeful and destructive."[2]

An interesting feature of the anger debate is how often it gets described dichotomously. Anger either is good or bad. It comes in one form or the other, and the implication is that it is straightforward to discern with which form we are dealing. But the very fact that the debate is dichotomous should make us think about the possibility that anger is more complicated. Further, we should worry that each camp focuses on only the form of anger that proves its side's point. As our earlier examples about how social activists can experience anger illustrate, we know from our own lives that anger comes in multiple forms. Further, we know that how we are experiencing anger can change even in the course of one setting. What may start as a flash of more instinctual, reactive anger can morph into anger intended to express moral outrage. Think of the quick anger that arises when you are driving slightly over the speed limit, and you see flashing lights and realize that a police officer is signaling for you to pull over. You are angry at being caught, even though you know you were driving over the speed limit. Depending on the setting, and on who the police officer is and who you are, your reactive anger may turn into moral outrage. You might realize that you actually were not pulled over for speeding, but have instead been pulled over for "driving while Black."

Anger also can morph over time. Consider a time when someone insulted you. Your first reaction may be to be angry at the personal harm that the insult caused. You confront the wrongdoer who apologizes, genuinely demonstrates remorse, and takes responsibility for their bad conduct. Even when you believe the wrongdoer is contrite, you hold onto your anger and it turns into anger that seeks revenge. Though the wrongdoer has taken good and reasonable steps to rectify

---

2. *Id.* at 12–13.

the harm they caused; you choose to hold onto your anger. You take your own harmful actions against the other person and justify your bad conduct based on the anger you have cultivated over time.

In each of the examples above, we likely can think of our own similar experiences. We also likely judged our own conduct at the time as justified or as misguided or as both. If we take a moment to reflect, we might also see that if we assume the examples were about another person's behavior, that may change how we judge the conduct. For example, we might criticize another person for holding onto anger and seeking revenge, whereas we rationalized our own behavior in that same setting. Or if we have not experienced routinized racial discrimination, we might be less willing to believe that a traffic stop warrants moral outrage. As we think about judging anger, we need to pay attention to features of anger laid out in the last chapter. We need to pay attention to the fact that anger has multiple forms, that it always is relational, and that it is socially constructed, including in ways that reflect power, bias, and control.

As we cultivate our capacity to prudentially judge anger, it will be helpful to look at the justifications from the anti-anger camp and pro-anger camp. We can then take those arguments and focus on the context of social activism to see how that helps us understand when or how anger is productive in social movement work.

Let's start with the anti-anger camp. Political philosopher Martha Nussbaum has offered an exemplary critique of anger.[3] Nussbaum accepts that anger is an inherent part of what it means for a person to have feelings. She recognizes that we all have embodied experiences that we label "anger." Her goal related to anger is not to erase it, but to focus on what the

---

3. *See* Martha Nussbaum, ANGER AND FORGIVENESS: RESENTMENT, GENEROSITY, JUSTICE (2016).

appropriate response is—both responding to another's anger and responding to our own anger. For Nussbaum, a constitutive feature of anger is that it includes a "payback wish." In other words, anger has feeling and framing rules that call on a person to react in some retributive or vengeful way. If you do something to me that makes me angry, that feeling means that you have wronged me in some way. Because I feel like I have been wronged, I will seek payback from you. Nussbaum sees anger's payback wish as backward-looking and always as a kind of tit-for-tat response. Anger is not designed to improve the situation going forward. Its only goal is to downgrade the wrongdoer. Thus, for Nussbaum, the payback wish unhelpfully "converts all injuries into problems of relative position. . . ." No one's lot is improved unless the other's lot is downgraded, and the "world . . . revolve[s] around the desire . . . for domination and control."[4]

Nussbaum readily acknowledges that anger can be a critical and powerful way for people to call out injustices. Further, she agrees that it is crucial for both personal and political discourse that there be a way to show and express injustice. She acknowledges there needs to be a way for members of a society to express concern for the dignity of themselves and others as well as express moral outrage at unjust acts or policies. But she also reminds us that protecting one person's or one group's dignity by denigrating another person or group is less worthy and less moral than protecting all dignitary interests.

As a way forward, Nussbaum offers the concept of "transition" anger whereby a person expresses anger at an injustice.[5] But the person is careful in crafting her response so that it looks forward and focuses on how to remedy the issue in a way that benefits all of society. Transition anger has a focused and limited purpose. It is a method to signal injustice

---

4. *Id.* at 29.
5. *Id.* at 35–37.

and to claim space for dignitary interests, but it is not meant as a solution to the wrongdoing. Transition anger may contain the seed of a payback wish, but anger should be set aside quickly enough that the need for revenge does not settle in. Ultimately for Nussbaum, "[t]he focus should be on establishing accountability for wrongdoing, as a crucial ingredient of building public trust, on expressing shared values, and then on moving beyond the whole drama of anger and forgiveness to forge attitudes that actually support trust and reconciliation."[6]

Nussbaum raises another concern about the consequences of anger's payback wish. In addition to worrying that payback focuses on harm, through revenge or retribution, instead of improving conditions for all, Nussbaum worries that anger imposes a burden on the person expressing it. Nussbaum considers the caustic nature of vengeful or retributive anger, and the risk that it becomes excessive and obsessive. Anger causes a person to become caught up in the backward-focused goal of paying back another, or the other side. As a consequence, a person becomes unable to consider the possibility of a way forward that would improve conditions for everyone. Anger no longer is a catalyst to help a person move towards a flourishing life. Instead, it becomes a "burdened virtue."[7]

The idea of a burdened virtue is particularly helpful as we think about the role of anger in social activism. As I described above, scholars and activists have repeatedly noted, and our own experiences of social activism have taught us, that anger is considered a key emotion in social activism. It may have moral goodness as an initial way of demanding dignity, and in that way, it can be virtuous. As Nussbaum notes, people in subordinated groups are "denied an equal status as knowers

---

6. *Id.* at 13.
7. Martha Nussbaum, *Victim Anger and Its Costs*, in ON ANGER, *supra* note 1 at 125.

and givers of testimony."[8] Nussbaum agrees that anger can help those in subordinated groups find their voices. It also can help those voices insist that their claims for space and time to be heard are legitimate and must be reckoned with by the dominant group. Anger can provide a way for those in subordinated groups to dismiss the dismissals of anger offered up by those in the dominant group.

For Nussbaum, the caustic side of anger in social activism is that it demands "a type of uncritical loyalty and solidarity."[9] Anger's burden on activists is that it calls for too much—the "other side" must always be distrusted. Once that is the required emotional labor, there is no space left for an activist to think about moving forward for mutual progress. Any overture to the other side is received by social movement colleagues as a betrayal, at worst, or as slipping back into learned, subordinated behaviors, at best. Nussbaum sees a way out of the burdens of anger through her concept of transition anger. Transition anger provides a mechanism for acknowledging anger's virtue of calling out an injustice. Importantly for those experiencing subordination, Nussbaum describes how transition anger can be a first response to the kinds of victim-blaming that dominant groups use as control methods. As Nussbaum describes, "Victim-blaming is ubiquitous as a strategy of subordination. It comes easy to the proud to construct fictions of their own moral superiority, portraying the subordinated as in some sense deserving their subordination because of intellectual and moral inferiority."[10] It is important to Nussbaum that people reclaim their fullest voices so that they are able to author their own choices with dignity and able to craft fulfilling lives.

---

8. *Id.* at 124.
9. *Id.*
10. *Id.* at 118.

Nonetheless, Nussbaum remains wary of anger. It is too easy for anger to become vengeful. It is too easy for the caustic side of anger to overwhelm the side of anger that helps a person find her voice. Within social movements, it is too easy for anger to become the only way in which movement colleagues can show loyalty and commitment. It becomes too easy for anger to replace a goal of improving society for all with a goal of punishing others.

How does the pro-anger camp respond to the worries of the anti-anger camp, and how does the pro-anger camp conceive of anger in ways that make it more positive than negative? Political philosopher Amia Srinivasan has deeply explored the idea of meritorious anger.[11] Like Nussbaum, Srinivasan posits that anger is a critical method for calling out injustice. Srinivasan offers the concept of "apt anger."[12] Anger is apt when it is a response to a moral wrong and when its expression is proportionate to the seriousness of the moral wrong. For example, if a colleague speaks to me disrespectfully, most of us would think my colleague's behavior was unjust. Thus, when I get angry, my anger expresses that I have been wronged morally. My anger is apt. If I then meet with my colleague and explain how I experienced her speech as disrespectful, and she genuinely apologizes, my anger remains apt if I move on from the incident. If I hold a grudge and bad-mouth my colleague for years, my anger no longer is apt because it has become disproportionate to the initial moral harm.

Apt anger also applies in larger societal contexts. It plays an important communicative role in society. It is a key way for a person to publicly express a moral harm and a social injustice. It both helps others see that a social injustice is occurring and it is an invitation to join in solidarity with the person

---

11. *See generally* Amia Srinivasan, *The Aptness of Anger*, 26 J. POL. PHIL. 123 (2018).

12. *Id.* at 126.

who is calling out the injustice. It matters not that there may be additional ways to call out injustice because calling out moral wrongs is intrinsically valuable—both for the person expressing apt anger and for society more generally.

Srinivasan takes on the anti-anger camp's charge that anger should be avoided because it is counterproductive. The counterproductivity charge posits that even if anger clearly and usefully signals and expresses that a moral harm has occurred, it does so in ways that, themselves, cause other harms or trigger reactions that are sufficiently unhelpful so that anger becomes counterproductive. For example, if my apt anger will trigger behaviors in others that put me and my family in physical danger, my anger, while still legitimately expressing a moral wrong, may create too much risk of harm. Srinivasan agrees that there are contexts in which apt anger will be counterproductive, including Nussbaum's concern about anger's payback wish.[13]

Srinivasan points out, however, that the counterproductivity charge often is levied in illegitimate ways. It often is levied by those in power against those experiencing subordination as a way to maintain control.[14] Think about the examples in the previous chapter about biased feeling and framing rules about anger. Translating some of those examples into Srinivasan's framework looks like this: Men can get angry because their anger is apt. But women's anger is counterproductive because they are shrill and irrational. Or an example like this: It might be true that there is racial discrimination in the U.S., but if people of color express that injustice through anger, it only makes things worse. When the counterproductivity charge is used like that, it is not actually a factual argument about the consequences of anger. It is a statement of bias and control. As a matter of factual description, it is highly unlikely

---

13. *Id.* at 131.
14. *Id.* at 133–34.

that the same behavior expressed by a man and by a woman will be more or less counterproductive, *but for* socially constructed rules about who can express what kinds of emotions. Thus, apt anger becomes even more important as a method of expressing, and protesting about, social injustices.

Srinivasan adds one more important observation in her defense of anger and the concern that it is counterproductive. She argues that when anger is apt, yet counterproductive, the person who is expressing apt anger is expected to be the one who changes their behavior. Srinivasan argues that causes an additional harm to the person calling out an injustice. They are told that while others might be permitted to express anger, they cannot do so because their anger is the wrong kind of emotional expression. That "affective injustice,"[15] as Srinivasan calls it, lays on top of the societal injustice that warranted the expression of apt anger in the first place.

The accounts of anger offered by Nussbaum and Srinivasan help us to see that anger is more complicated, and more interesting, than the dichotomous assessment of "anger is good" versus "anger is bad." In fact, while Nussbaum and Srinivasan have been identified with opposite camps in the anger debate, each of them acknowledges some key features about anger raised by the other side. Both strongly agree that injustice must be called out, and that anger is well understood as a method for signaling moral harm. Both agree that anger can go too far. It can become vengeful. It can be expressed in a way that is disproportionate to the harm or in a way that does not respect genuine efforts of a wrongdoer to repair the harm. Both are wary about the ways in which those in power can misuse anger to maintain control—either by directly using anger as control over someone or by inappropriately disclaiming another person's justly expressed anger.

---

15. *Id.* at 135.

The challenge, then, for activists is how to discern and navigate anger in social movement work so that it is more effective than not. Activists have difficult choices that often require them to trade off between equally compelling values. For example, we have learned that internally to a movement, anger motivates. It brings new activists to a movement. It helps movement colleagues experience loyalty and solidarity with each other even if they have not worked together before or do not have existing relationships with each other. Anger reflects values about the importance of finding a like-minded community where one can feel certain about finding support and empathy. Anger reflects values about steadfastness, especially in the face of opposition. Those values lead to positive results for social movements and help movements build and keep momentum.

At the same time, anger is caustic and can be hurtful internally to a movement. It can cause activists to judge each other too harshly—"She doesn't seem angry enough about the wrong happening to us. She must not really be committed to our work and we shouldn't trust her." That can trigger an unhelpful cycle where activists feel like they have to continually increase their anger in order to convince each other that they are genuine about their work or sufficiently committed to the work. If that happens, the important values that anger is supposed to serve get lost. Anger is not in service of community building or shared empathy. Anger becomes unmoored from those positive values.

Similarly, external to the movement, anger is a key communication tool used to signal to others that an injustice has been (or is) occurring. Further, when a dominant group has created feeling and framing rules for anger that turn it into an instrument of power and control, reclaiming anger is a key mechanism for a subordinated group to refuse to comply. Thus, anger positively serves values related to dignity and respect. It serves the positive value of making an injustice transparent. It also serves the positive value of resisting subordination.

But anger also unhelpfully encourages activists to see those outside of their movement only as enemies. Anger's payback wish means that a dignitary harm continues to be inflicted, instead of creating change that is mutually beneficial and protects all dignitary interests. Thus, activists fail to make connections with others with whom they may share common ground. Without making connections, activists miss options for mutual gain, not only for their own movement, but for gains that cross movements or bring in other allies.

It may seem like an activist has a fundamental starting choice to make about anger—either to adopt it or forego it. Both the pro-anger and the anti-anger camps believe forcefully in their views. I would suggest each view underappreciates the detriments to its side. I also would suggest that each view oversubscribes to a view of anger as a "hot" emotion. In other words, the feeling rules for anger in social movement work emphasize displays that are voluble, ardent, and public. It is to that perception of public resistance that I turn to next.

3

Public Resistance[1]

THUS FAR, AS I HAVE DESCRIBED social movement work and protest, my examples have focused on public acts. The angry mob, the stalwart protestor, and the defiant protestor all perform their acts of resistance in public. In fact, for most of us, it may seem odd to suggest that social movement resistance would be something other than public. Isn't the point of a social movement to call out an injustice and make it apparent to others? I think that quick reaction captures an important feature of the role of public resistance in social movement work—that we presume it to be the best method, maybe even the only effective method, for activists to call out injustices and put others on notice that change will be pressed for. We presume that publicness is critical for a variety of reasons. Some reasons are instrumental. For example, public protest broadly gets the word out. It is a straightfor-

---

1. Some portions of this chapter previously appeared in Deborah J. Cantrell, *Silence, Protest and Lawyering*, 22 RUTGERS J. L. & RELIGION 84 (2021).

ward method of widely announcing an injustice is occurring, which helps bring others into the movement and helps catalyze sympathy from others. Further, we presume that public protest serves important dignitary interests. As we already have considered, speaking out publicly about an injustice feels empowering and is a way of claiming respect for one's experience. Speaking out publicly also can be a way to reclaim one's agency in the face of subordination—"You can't tell me to be quiet about this harm. I claim my right and ability to speak up for myself, and to speak up in the ways that I feel are best."

All of those reasons make sense, and we likely can come up with ready examples of public protest that illustrate each reason. In fact, the ease with which we think about protest as necessarily public may make it seem inapt to even pose a query about nonpublic protest or resistance. Such a thing might exist, but how could it possibly matter? This chapter takes up that inquiry. It first considers why we so soundly think of resistance in its public form. It next considers the unhelpful consequences of seeing resistance as necessarily requiring public actions. It concludes by exploring the idea of internal resistance or a resistance of quietude, and considering how that form of resistance can benefit social activists and their movement work.

As I noted above, there is an intuitive sense that social movement work must have some form of public resistance. By the time a group has formed with sufficient solidarity and focus to think of itself as a social movement, people have expended quite a bit of energy, including emotional labor. At some point, the group decides that it wants its energy to matter beyond itself. Emotional labor accumulates something like this. First, there is an individual's emotional labor to become aware of an injustice, to think through and understand its contours, and to become aware that the injustice was not just directed at one individual. Next, it takes energy and emotional labor for individuals to find each other, and build sufficient connections so that they discover shared experiences related to the injustice. Then, it takes emotional labor to build trust and solidarity within a group. For some groups, their primary purpose may be to provide support and a safe space for group members to speak about their experiences. It can be both relieving and empowering to be able to express a full range of emotions about an injustice that you have experienced without worrying that those around you will judge you, dismiss you, or punish you.

For some groups, though, there comes a time when the group decides to make its grievance publicly known and to call for change. There are a range of factors that can move a group into public resistance. For some, it may be access to new resources, like money, which helps the group decide it is ready for public resistance. Money can help with things as simple as buying materials to make signs, as well as with more complicated issues like setting up bail funds for group members who get arrested. For other groups, it may be a charismatic leader who steps forward and is willing to take the public lead. In the U.S., we can think readily of charismatic movement leaders both across time and across a spectrum of issues. It may be a notable event that makes a group feel it must become public about its resistance. Again, examples come readily to mind across history from the Triangle Shirtwaist Factory fire in 1911 to the Stonewall Inn riot in 1969 and to the current Black Lives Matter movement spurred by the acquittal of George Zimmerman in 2012. It also can be a combination of any or all of those factors that prompts a group to move into public resistance.

The point of the above examples is to highlight how easy and familiar it is for us to think about resistance in social movement work as being public. Just like we quickly think about anger as a primary motivating emotion in activist work, we have equally ready ideas about what actions count as resistance. To be an activist means that your protest and resistance to an injustice are public and known. Once a group has decided to take public action—to become activists—that triggers expectations both within the group, and outside of it, about what conduct is expected. Within an activist group, members who are loud and out in front are valorized. Being publicly out front means a member is really committed to the cause. Ardency is *the way* a member shows her loyalty. Those outside the group also expect an activist to show her commitment by being loud and out front. But an activist's ardency is seen as proof that group members are irrational, unpredictable, and potentially dangerous.

To be clear, I am not claiming that resistance can only be public. There are a myriad of ways in which resistance gets demonstrated outside of the public sphere. Political scientist James C. Scott has described the tactics of non-public resistance as "hidden transcripts."[2] Scott's idea of hidden transcripts captures the ways in which subordinated groups manipulate the behaviors expected of them by the dominant group. For example, if the dominant group expects members of a subordinated group to act deferentially, a person may choose to act particularly deferentially as a display of subtle resistance and mockery. As Scott has put it: "What may look from above like the extraction of a required performance can easily look from below like the artful manipulation of deference and flattery to achieve its own ends."[3] Hidden transcripts of resistance can encompass a wide range of behaviors that are intended to push against subordination, yet in low-profile ways that may reduce the risk of retaliation or punishment. Thus, non-public resistance is practical, strategic, and a critical way of subtly commandeering the meaning of expected behaviors.

---

2. *See* James C. Scott, DOMINATION AND THE ARTS OF RESISTANCE: HIDDEN TRANSCRIPTS (1990).

3. *Id.* at 34.

We also see non-public resistance in settings that are less about power and control between groups of people. A ready example is the way in which a person can make choices about what goods she purchases and consumes as a way of expressing resistance. A person who is concerned about concentrated animal farming operations may refuse to purchase meat from large-scale, commercial producers. She intends those choices as resistance even though she does not announce that intention to the person who checks her out at the grocery store. If the consumer were to disclose her purchasing choices to others and describe them as her way of protesting against inhumane animal practices, I think most of us would agree that the consumer's actions count as protest.

Nonetheless, while we may be aware of hidden transcripts, and as social activists, we may practice a range of non-public resistance strategies, we hold on to the utopian ideal of "speaking truth to power." In many ways, we have constructed an ideal of true and authentic resistance as necessarily public. Further, once we think about public protest, we quickly have to confront explicit "transcripts" about protest. As James C. Scott and others have illuminated, it serves those in power to be seen as tolerating some level of disagreement and protest. Controlled and constrained protest allows those in power to create a transcript or narrative that they listen to all members of the community. In the U.S., we have a version of that narrative that says that our democracy is founded on the idea that everyone's voice should be heard. A society makes the best choices when all ideas have a chance of equally competing in the marketplace or public square. Thus, democracy thrives when it respects protest.

Despite that narrative of tolerating protest, those in power constrain protest in order to blunt its impact. For example, as labor law scholar Ahmed White has demonstrated, the right to strike, as a means of worker protest, has been degraded over time.[4] White argues that the early history of strikes included worker actions that were sufficiently disruptive that employers had to take the striking workers seriously. But over time, labor laws were amended to constrain what actions constituted lawful striking, thereby muting the impact of a strike on employers. The amended labor laws were justified on the grounds of maintaining public safety and protecting property, and not as a way of constraining workers' voices protesting labor conditions. White argues, however, that the true purpose was to preserve employer power over workers. Employers understood the need to preserve some form of strike in order to be able to argue that they respected democracy and the marketplace of ideas, even when their real goal was to control workers and restrain dissent.

Similarly, think about more prosaic ways in which protest can be constrained. Most towns and cities have permitting requirements for "special events," and special events include everything from farmers' markets to arts and crafts fairs and marches or rallies. What gets subtly signaled by that inclusive list is that all the events are of the same kind—a friendly gathering of community members strolling along the public square together. Of course, we also know that marches, rallies, and other kinds of protest do receive particular protection from government restrictions under the U.S. Constitution's First Amendment. That makes them different from a farmers' market or a craft fair, and requires that a government entity justify its regulations more carefully and thoroughly than it needs to for non-First Amendment activities. Nonetheless, it serves those in power to foster notions of special events as being best for the community when they have the feel of a farmers' market on a sunny weekend morning.

---

4. Ahmed White, *Its Own Dubious Battle: The Impossible Defense of an Effective Right to Strike*, 2018 WISC. L. REV. 1665 (2018).

As noted above, that controlling dynamic is not necessarily improved by identifying a "right" to political speech. A "right" to free speech is constructed and controlled by those in power just like a "right" to strike. Our society describes the Constitutionally-created right to free speech in more powerful terms than the statutorily-created right to strike. For example, we often hear the right to free speech described as fundamental and a core protected liberty of living in American society. But it is those in power, in the courts and in local, state, and federal governments across the country, who decide how much protection any one person's, or group's, speech actually will receive. Rights are not imbued with their own magical enforcement powers. Ordinary people, with their privileges, biases, and beliefs, enforce rights. As critical scholar Ratna Kapur has commented: "Rights are not bulwarks of defence against state power, but are a crucial aspect of power's aperture and governmentality—in other words, rights can *themselves* be tactics and vehicles of governance and domination. . . ."[5]

Social activists are aware of both the ideal of speaking truth to power and the ways in which those in power orchestrate seemingly neutral restrictions on protest that are designed to blunt its impact. As a result, just like there are reasons for activists to reclaim the rightness of expressing emotions like anger, there are reasons for activists to reclaim the rightness of vigorous public resistance. Especially for activists who are protesting subordination, it can be empowering to move beyond the hidden transcripts of resistance to a clear, uncompromising public transcript that rejects subordination. Part of that rejection can include refusing to politely protest within the constraints insisted upon by those in power. For example, when some activists in the Black Lives Matter movement found it

---

5. Ratna Kapur, GENDER, ALTERITY AND HUMAN RIGHTS: FREEDOM IN A FISHBOWL 35 (2018).

hard to get permits to protest on city streets, they strategically chose to stage an unpermitted protest blockading a busy highway. As one activist described the strategy: "It's definitely more effective to do the marches without a permit because, one, the point is to disrupt the status quo and if we had a permitted march it would look like a parade and not a protest; two, it doesn't make sense to go through the police who are part of the system of racism that we are challenging."[6]

Activists also understand that those in power stand ready to deploy the trope of the angry, unruly mob even when public resistance is peaceful but intentionally disruptive, like the highway blockades. For example, some Minnesota lawmakers supported legislation to increase penalties for protestors who blocked highways. Protestors were portrayed as rabble-rousers intent on destroying property and causing other kinds of damage that caused cities and counties to waste their tax dollars for cleaning up afterwards.[7] The dynamic in play moves in one way, with each side ratcheting its responses upward. Those in power seek to control or delegitimate those protesting. In response, protestors show up more vigorously in order to clearly demonstrate they will not acquiesce. In response, those in power escalate their own efforts, and so on. The only resistance that fits into such a cycle is hot, angry, public protest that is quick and ardent.

Further, activists respond not only to those trying to control them, but also to other related social movements. It can matter to activists what their peers think of their protest efforts. Often times, activists judge each other's commitment to the cause by how willing a group is to vigorously protest. For

6. Zaid Jilani, *Minnesota Is Trying to Crush Black Lives Movement Highway Protests, A Tactic Activists Have Used for Decades*, The Intercept (April 5, 2017, 3:38 PM), https://theintercept.com/2017/04/05/minnesota-is-trying -to-crush-black-lives-movement-highway-protests-a-tactic-activists-have -used-for-decades/ (quoting Moumita Ahmed).

7. *Id.*

example, when Phillip Randolph, Roy Wilkins, and Martin Luther King, Jr. were planning the 1963 March on Washington with a commitment to nonviolence and peaceful protest, Malcolm X was critical of those efforts because the protest "ceased to be angry, ceased to be hot, [and] it ceased to be uncompromising."[8] Or in the environmental movement, Greenpeace, with its commitment to strident direct action, positively contrasts itself to other groups, like the "mild-mannered, middle-aged Sierra Club. . . ."[9] Thus, activists can feel pressure towards hot, public protest in order to prove their legitimacy with social movement work—"We are *real* activists because we get out into the streets immediately."

With all of the above pressures on activists to think about resistance in its most ardently public form, it is easy to forget to consider other ways to cultivate resistance. As I noted already, resistance can take the less public form of hidden transcripts, where a person acts publicly in ways they intend as resistance, but the actions are less overt and can elide the perception of resistance. I think that kind of hidden resistance is familiar to social activists, but considered less impactful than robust public resistance. But, activists appreciate that hidden resistance may be a person's only choice, especially if a person feels like they are acting on their own. Part of the point of creating a movement is to create a group of people who can provide some safety and some anonymity for each other. Thus, one of the points of a movement is to create a structure that allows less overt resistance to blossom into public and assertive resistance. Again, publicness is the priority.

The form of resistance that I think is unfamiliar to social activists is an internal form, cultivated by an individual within themselves through quietude, contemplation, and revelation.

---

8. Malcolm X, *Message to the Grassroots*, in MALCOLM X SPEAKS: SELECTED SPEECHES AND STATEMENTS 16 (George Breitman ed., 1965).

9. Jan Noel, *Greenpeace: The First Fifty Years*, PEACE MAGAZINE, October–December 2020 at 6.

For many, the idea of quiet resistance is, itself, a contradiction because "quiet" is understood as "silent," and silence is understood as a failure to resist. To be silent is to fail to speak out about an injustice. Therefore, to be quiet and internal must mean that a person is failing to resist.

But that equation of "quiet=silence=failure to resist" is not fully accurate. Scholar Kevin Quashie has illuminated a more fulsome, rich understanding of quiet in his research that can help us see the generative possibilities of quiet. Quashie encourages us to think about quiet not as an absence of something, like sound or thoughts, but as "space of interrogation"[10] that can help foster an "astuteness about living"[11] that need not be bounded by constraints a person experiences in the external world. For Quashie, the interior life provides spaciousness to investigate the pressures of social identities and how identities can build habits of responding. The interior is not limited by external identities, yet it also is aware of injustice and the consequences of identities. As Quashie describes it: "To ask about the freedom within is to reimagine the collective such that the inclination to stand up for yourself is no longer limited to responding to the actions of others. . . . Standing up for yourself is not oppositional, but abundant."[12] Quashie is not saying that resisting unjust social rules is unimportant or that a person should be able to ignore prejudices. Instead, I understand him to be insisting that people's lives, particularly those experiencing subordination, are entitled to be imagined and lived in ways that go beyond the expectation that the most important feature of subordination is the right (and necessity) to protest publicly.

Quashie worries that constructing a social identity around public resistance actually serves the dominant culture. For

---

10. Kevin Quashie, THE SOVEREIGNTY OF QUIET: BEYOND RESISTANCE IN BLACK CULTURE 134 (2012).
11. *Id.* at 49.
12. *Id.* at 100.

example, it allows the dominant culture to maintain false constructions like the "dangerous" Black man or woman. The dominant culture constructs "blackness" to require public resistance. Then, the dominant culture insists that a Black person's public resistance must be seen as threatening, not liberating. As Quashie puts it:

> Constructions of blackness-as-resistance, then, serve the needs and fantasies of the dominant culture. And yet it is difficult to dismiss resistance entirely, since it is a legitimate framework for understanding some aspects of black experience and has been readily embraced by black people. No, the problem is not resistance or the notion of public expressiveness per se, but the way in which these notions have become the dominant perspectives for thinking about blackness.[13]

Quashie's liberatory move, then, is to embrace the interior world for its ability to foster imaginations beyond the reactive script of public resistance. Quashie hopes that those experiencing subordination can imagine themselves having agency for acts in addition to public resistance. I think Quashie's reflections invite social activists to inquire in what ways social change might be spurred forward other than through hot, overt acts of public resistance.

But Quashie's invitation can only be taken up by easing our grip on a firmly held conception that angry public resistance is *the way* to express and preserve dignity. That is hard to do, and validly so. As we already have considered, there are important dignitary goals that are served by angry public resistance. It is a clear way to reclaim agency over the meaning of emotions and over the right to express emotions. It also is a clear way to signal that a moral harm is being perpetrated upon protestors, and should be stopped. To step back from

---

13. *Id.* at 129.

angry public resistance feels like ceding ground and feels like acquiescing to subordination.

We may be willing to acknowledge the other kinds of dignitary interests that Quashie reminds us about, including the dignitary interest in creating a sense of self that is not always defined in response to the dominant culture, and the dignitary interest in having an interior, reflective life that does not have to be made public in order to have worth. But we may not be clear enough about the positive and beneficial consequences of those interior dignitary interests to be willing to set down angry public resistance as the presumptively correct way to make social change. So it is useful to more fully consider the beneficial consequences of contemplative silence.

First, we need to have a more nuanced understanding of quiet and silence. We often think of quiet and silence in terms of absence—the absence of sound, the absence of distractions, or the absence of activity. Or we think of silence and quiet as conditions that are imposed on us for some other reason. We are told to be quiet because someone else is speaking. We are told to be silent in order to be able to hear an important message from someone else. We are told to be quiet so that we are not distracting from some other activities.

But silence and quietude also are affirmatively good. Quashie describes a person's interior reservoir as a place of "self-fullness."[14] Instead of understanding silence and quiet as being spaces of absence, we can see them as spaces of potential. Importantly, their potential is not linear and goal-directed. In other words, unlike public spaces of action, where there are expectations about what conduct is, or is not, acceptable, the interior spaces of silence and quiet are free of such expectations. If a person can cultivate silence and quiet well, the space becomes the wellspring for the un-thought-of, the unexpected, and the unforeseen. Silence and quiet become

---

14. *Id.* at 121.

transformative. Instead of understanding silence and quiet as about rest and not-thinking and non-action, we see the space as active and transformative. As Quashie puts it: "Quiet helps us to understand the activism involved in being aware, in paying attention, in considering."[15]

Faith traditions offer another, related way of understanding the generative potential for silence. For example, Abrahamic traditions have the concept of "listening for God." To listen for God is to be open to revelation. A person listens with an openness of mind, not knowing what she may hear, or whether the questions she hopes will be answered, in fact, will be the ones to which a revelation is addressed. Silence is the practice through which deep discernment can occur. In other words, it is a state of readiness, not an action in response to something else. I am not being silent because of someone else's actions; I am being silent in order to place myself in the best possible condition to hear and learn something beyond myself. The Catholic theologian Thomas Merton described the generative possibilities of silent contemplation this way:

> [It] must provide an area, a space of liberty, of silence, in which possibilities are allowed to surface and new choices—beyond routine choice—become manifest. It should create a new experience of time, not as stopgap stillness, but a "temps vierge"—not a blank to be filled or an untouched space to be conquered and violated, but a space which can enjoy its own potentialities and hopes—and its own presence to itself.[16]

Of course, for most faith traditions, the point of silent contemplation or quietude focuses on a religious outcome—to receive wisdom from God. That goal may or may not be relevant for social movement work, but the process and practic-

---

15. *Id.* at 72.
16. Thomas Merton, THE ASIAN JOURNAL OF THOMAS MERTON 117 (1968).

es related to "listening for God" are very germane. The open and inquisitive mindset required for revelation is one that encourages imagination and receptivity to the unexpected. It is not a mindset that focuses on a specific answer for a specific conundrum. Instead, it holds the conundrum up with the hope that some vantage point that has been missed, or some new facet of the challenge, will be revealed. In turn, those revelations will themselves illuminate pathways to navigate the conundrum that had been hidden and unknown.

Another key consequence of revelatory, contemplative practices is the experience often described in faith traditions as "oneness." That is the idea that quiet contemplation is not designed to wall off the world so that a person focuses solely on themselves. Instead, it creates a setting in which one becomes fully aware of the interconnectedness of all life, and sees oneself as necessarily interdependent with others. Buddhism offers an eloquent example of the idea of "oneness." The Buddha is believed to have offered the following teaching: "This is, because that is. This is not, because that is not. This comes to be, because that comes to be. This ceases to be, because that ceases to be."[17] The teaching is not intended to be paradoxical or puzzling. It is intended to capture simply how all things are interconnected. In many ways, it is the same lesson as is posed by the query: "Which comes first, the chicken or the egg?"

Critically, any starting connection with another can be initially perceived along different dimensions. There are connections that we expect to be positive, such as between good friends. There are connections that we expect to be negative, such as with a workplace rival. There are connections that we expect to be neutral, such as the brief connection we have when we make eye contact with another driver on the road

17. Thich Nhat Hanh, THE HEART OF THE BUDDHA'S TEACHING: TRANSFORMING SUFFERING INTO PEACE, JOY AND LIBERATION 221 (Broadway Books, 1998).

with us. Through contemplative practices, as we let our minds become more open and aware, and we push beyond habituated perceptions, we see that our starting assumptions about any kind of connection are partial. Good friends have times when they fall out and feel negatively towards each other. Workplace rivals can become close collaborators when the full work group has to step up for success. The driver next to us can trigger anger or gratitude from us depending on what actions the driver takes. In other words, the practice of "oneness" teaches us an important feature of human relationality—its only constant is interdependent change.

Initially, the idea of constant change in relationships may feel negative. I want to be able to count on the constancy of a friendship. Or, as a social activist, I want to be able to count on loyalty from the other activists in my group. It is not comforting to think that relationships always are changing because change puts my relationships at risk. However, faith traditions see interdependence as hopeful, not as full of vagary. By understanding that we all are interconnected, that encourages us to see ourselves in others, and to see the possibility of common ground regardless of change. As religious scholar, Karen Armstrong, has described it, the major faith traditions across the world "share an ideal of sympathy, respect, and universal concern."[18] The relationality that is revealed through silence and quietude is radical because it insists that we see connections between ourselves regardless of harmony or discord. I am in relationship with everyone with whom I have contact whether that contact is positive or negative. Further, I stay in relationship with everyone with whom I have contact regardless of how that contact changes. I am in relationship with the person I call "friend" both when our relationship is harmonious and when it is in conflict.

---

18. Karen Armstrong, THE GREAT TRANSFORMATION: THE BEGINNING OF OUR RELIGIOUS TRADITIONS 466 (Anchor Books, 2006).

To use a Buddhist frame, using silence as a way to cultivate an open, inquiring mind allows me to move beyond the constant, habituated chatter in my mind. I begin to hear instead a richer and more complicated tapestry of sounds in the world—whether that is the joy of laughter, the cry of loss, words of care, or the bite of words spoken in anger or hate. I cannot pick and choose what I hear, and because of that, I am able to move beyond my own self-interested perspective. I realize that I have no choice about experiencing the fullest range of radical relationality—positive, negative, or neutral. Instead, my choices are about how I navigate that relationality and how I learn to do so skillfully.

I think an understanding of constant relational change is profoundly missing in social activism—by activists, by those in opposition, and by those who are observers. The relational lines are rigid. You are with us or against us. You are a troublemaker or you are a good member of society. We quickly draw those relational lines, and we hold fast to them. Prioritizing public resistance only amplifies line drawing, largely because we also prioritize public resistance in its ardent, hot form. To stand with us or against us can be literal—my line of people physically standing in opposition to your line of people. Because ardent public resistance expects rigid relational lines, it is fairly intolerant of relational change even as it seeks social change. An activist who does not protest in expected ways risks being called out as disloyal or uncommitted. An activist who reaches across relational lines risks being ostracized as a traitor. On the other side, an observer who speaks sympathetically about protestors is called out as "soft" and insufficiently concerned about the "good people" in town. To go back to the earlier discussion about emotional labor, ardent public resistance has feeling and framing rules that are about maintaining separation between groups and seeing only difference between insiders and outsiders.

How might transformative silence help change that dynamic? Are there ways that social activists might learn from the practices in faith traditions about listening for God and welcoming interconnectedness between people? How would those faith-based lessons need to be reframed in order to disrupt current commitments to ardent, public protest? It is to those questions that the next chapter turns.

4

Fierce Love and Abiding Love

AS NOTED IN THE EARLIER CHAPTERS, there are important, anti-subordination interests that are in play for activists
as they think through strategies and actions for their social
movements. Before activists will consider changing or adding strategies, they will need to be convinced that any new
strategy will benefit the movement. If there is something to be
gained from faith-based transformative practices that commit
to radical relationality, we first need to better understand what
rules social activists currently have about relationality. Then
we need to compare those rules to those of faith-based rules
about radical relationality. If we discover that the two sets of
rules do not have much overlap, that prompts two follow-up
questions. The first is to assess and confirm that there would
be genuine benefits to activists if they adopted faith-based
practices about radical relationality. If there are, then the
second question is whether there are ways to reframe radical
relationality practices so that they resonate for activists. This
chapter takes up those inquiries.

Just like we did with anger, it will be helpful to consider how the emotion of love is understood more generally. Like anger, love has many emotional instantiations. It has a quick reflexive form, like the burst of pleasure we feel when something delights us—"Oh! I love that sunset." It has a form that relates to close, personal relationships such as with family members or longtime friends. It has forms related to intimate relationships, including a more reflexive form that we think of as infatuation, and a longer term form that we think of as a deep abiding with another. Finally, like anger, love also has a form that signals moral values, and is used as a shorthand way of saying that something matters to a person because it represents a value choice. For example, activists working to end large commercial animal slaughtering facilities talk about their love of all living beings and how that requires them to protest inhumane and unjust treatment towards animals.

Similar to anger, love has socially constructed feeling and framing rules. Many of those rules are prosaic. Love, in all of its forms, should generate positive feelings and connections. I am supposed to feel happy when I see my best friend. I should smile and greet her warmly. I am supposed to remember important dates in my intimate relationship and take actions that show my partner that I continue to love her. Of course, like all feeling and framing rules, we always have a choice about whether to comply with them. If my best friend did something that I felt was a slight, I might not greet her so warmly. I am breaching feeling and framing rules as a way of signaling to her that I believe she also breached those same rules when she slighted me.

At its core, however, we expect "love" to mean a positive connection. Thus, when we think about the idea of "love" as it relates to larger groups, like social movements, it is easy to understand how there are rules that result in clear lines being drawn between "us" and "them." As an activist, if I describe the commitment I have to my cause in terms of love, part of what I am saying is that I have a moral value that is not shared by those outside of my movement. I oppose concentrated animal feeding operations because of my love for all living beings. I believe that the people who operate such facilities could only do so because they do not share my value of love for all living beings. I am on one side; they are on the other. As such, the relationality between my side and their side is antagonistic, and thus, does not fit into any concept of love.

When we look at social movements, we can see the same either-or, us-them, relational dynamic in play. Within a movement, relationality is important and positive. Activists want to feel connected to each other. Activists want to be able to trust each other. Activists find support and strength knowing that others in their group have mutual experiences of the injustice that brought each of them into their social justice work. Relationality within a movement helps stave off feelings of isolation that a person experiencing injustice may have. It helps an activist stay motivated—"I have to keep up this work. My movement colleagues are depending on me." All of those emotional commitments feel similar to the ones we expect when we are talking about the kind of love between close groups of friends. But like anger in activism, which gets oversimplified to its ardent, public form, "love" in movement work gets oversimplified into a form that I have called hyper-loyalty.[1] There is a false bright line—either you are with us or you are against us. Because there inevitably can be disagreements on the margins about what counts as "with us" or "against us," an activist gets pushed toward actions that can clearly be understood as loyal. An activist has to overperform emotions that signal her commitment to the social movement so as to protect herself from charges of disloyalty or lackadaisical commitment.

---

1. *See* Deborah J. Cantrell, *Lawyers, Loyalty, and Social Change*, 89 DEN. UNIV. L. REV. 941 (2012).

The pressure to show hyper-loyalty also causes an activist to overperform her lack of relationality to those outside the movement. Or, to put it another way, hyper-loyalty causes an activist to overperform hostile relationships with those outside the movement. In order to show loyalty to the movement, an activist treats outsiders with extreme distrust. The only relational possibility is "enemy." To be open to the possibility of any common ground with someone outside the movement is read by activist colleagues as capitulating to the other side. Even working with another activist group can be fraught. As can be seen in the earlier examples of Malcolm X's criticism of Martin Luther King, Jr.'s plans for the March on Washington and Greenpeace's criticism of the Sierra Club, activist groups often disagree with each other. That disagreement breeds distrust, and that distrust amplifies the pattern that positive relationality is preserved for those within one's group, and hostile relationality is presumed for those outside.

As we think about whether activists might even be willing to consider practices from faith traditions, a starting challenge is that activists practice patterns of emotional relationality that do not easily line up with faith-based practices of radical relationality in which all persons are interconnected. That challenge is made harder by the fact that many faith traditions describe their commitments to interconnectedness using the word "love." For example, in Abrahamic traditions, one is taught to "love thy neighbor." In Christian traditions, there are many lessons about the boundless and unconditional love that Jesus showed. In Buddhism, there are dedicated practices to cultivate lovingkindness and compassion for all living beings. Given that our prominent emotional constructions of love focus on affirming relationships—"good" relationships—describing radical relationality as love can be disorienting. Why should I have to love my neighbor when he blares his music at all hours no matter how many times I ask him to turn down the volume? My neighbor's behavior is selfish and I should not have to pretend otherwise. Why should I show unconditional love, as Jesus might have, to a racist white supremacist who is marching down my town's street? Prejudice is a moral wrong that must be called out.

Is there a way forward that can address the valid queries above? I think there is. As scholars, theologians, and those who are faithful have explored, in many religious traditions the idea of love is more capacious than our typical social constructions of love. Faith-based ideals of love call on people to meet each other with the same kind of open and curious mind as does listening for God. Through that open and curious stance, we necessarily learn that all of us are connected in some way. The consequence of acknowledging those interconnections is that we must move towards one another instead of closing ourselves off. As a person of faith might say, "To see myself, is to see another. To see another is to see myself."

Critically, however, acknowledging interconnection is not the same as agreeing with the other person. The core foundational *fact* of radical relationality is that it *describes* the world; it does not *judge* it. Faith-based traditions accept that descriptive fact, and then offer up practices to respond to that fact. In all traditions, "love of neighbor" is not apologetic. To acknowledge interconnectedness does not also require us to excuse, ignore, or apologize for morally bad behavior. Dr. Martin Luther King, Jr. spoke often about this particular kind of "love" that pushes for change. As he described it:

> In speaking of love . . . we are not referring to some sentimental or affectionate emotion. It would be nonsense to urge men to love their oppressors in an affectionate sense. Love in this connection [of social change] means understanding, redemptive good will. When we speak of loving those who oppose us, we refer to neither *eros* nor *philia*; we speak of a love which is expressed in

the Greek word *agape*. . . . *Agape* is disinterested love. It is a love in which the individual seeks not his own good, but the good of his neighbor (1 Cor. 10:24). *Agape* does not begin by discriminating between worthy and unworthy people, or any qualities people possess. . . . *Agape* is not a weak, passive love. It is love in action. *Agape* is love seeking to preserve and create community. It is insistence on community even when one seeks to break it. . . . In the final analysis, *agape* means a recognition of the fact that all life is interrelated. All humanity is involved in a single process, and all men are brothers.[2]

The practice that Dr. King created to put *agape* into action was nonviolent resistance, or what he called "love in action." Through protest marches, lunch counter sit-ins, workers' strikes, and boycotts, activists demonstrated the fact of interconnectedness. They were a part of the larger community, regardless of whether the dominant white community believed, agreed, or treated activists as belonging. In King's words, activists insisted on equal membership in the community, even if that meant activists would first need to break the current order of the existing community. Importantly, the point of breaking community was not revenge. It was not anger's payback wish that motivated King's nonviolent resistance. It was the possibility that interconnectedness would provide a path forward to change.

As motivating and inspiring as Dr. King was, there were civil rights activists who remained skeptical of, and even hostile to, nonviolent resistance. Dr. King's most notable critic, Malcolm X, regularly criticized Dr. King's commitment to nonviolence, finding it an untenable way to bring about social change. In comparing Dr. King's approach (the "Negro

---

2. Martin Luther King, Jr., *An Experiment in Love*, in A TESTAMENT OF HOPE: THE ESSENTIAL WRITINGS AND SPEECHES OF MARTIN LUTHER KING, JR. 19–20 (James M. Washington ed., 1986).

revolution") to his separatist approach, Malcom X had this to say about the Negro revolution:

> . . . [Y]ou don't have a peaceful revolution. You don't have a turn-the-other-cheek revolution. There's no such thing as a nonviolent revolution. The only kind of revolution that is nonviolent is the Negro revolution. The only revolution in which the goal is loving your enemy is the Negro revolution. It's the only revolution in which the goal is a desegregated lunch counter, a desegregated theater, a desegregated park, and a desegregated public toilet; you can sit down next to white folks—on the toilet. That's no revolution.[3]

I think the disagreement between Dr. King and Malcolm X demonstrates some of the key dynamics that are created by hyper-loyalty. Hyper-loyalty privileges distrusting those outside of one's own movement. That can include distrusting other groups that work on the same social justice issue, but in different ways or with different priorities. Further, the distrust that hyper-loyalty cultivates is not passive. In other words, an activist is expected to affirmatively build walls between herself and those outside of her movement. The practice is the opposite of interconnection. It is active disconnection. Considering the strenuousness of hyper-loyalty, it is hard to discern how a message of radical relationality could ever be seeded.

To further complicate the setting, just as anger has its apt form, hyper-loyalty can be seen by activists as serving justifiable and important goals. Movement work is hard. Most strategy choices and action choices have to be made in the face of uncertainty. It often is not clear what the right choice is because there often are several plausible options. Colleagues within a movement need to trust that there is a safe space for

---

3. Malcolm X, *Message to the Grassroots*, in MALCOLM X SPEAKS: SELECTED SPEECHES AND STATEMENTS 9 (George Breitman ed., 1965).

candid and vulnerable conversations, and that those conversations will be kept confidential and inside the group. Hyperloyalty helps create those safe spaces. Malcolm X articulated this need as follows:

> Instead of airing our differences in public, we have to realize we're all the same family. And when you have a family squabble, you don't get out on the sidewalk. If you do, everyone calls you uncouth, unrefined, uncivilized, savage. If you don't make it at home, you settle it at home . . . argue it out behind closed doors, and then when you come out on the street, you pose a common front, a united front.[4]

Hyper-loyalty is a mechanism that protects a group from unhelpfully exposing itself to criticism and attacks from those opposing the group. The challenge, however, is that hyper-loyalty, like anger, often is expressed in its most ardent form. Activists may too readily describe anyone outside the movement as an enemy, and may too readily chastise those within the movement as being disloyal when they suggest reaching across movement boundaries. Hyper-loyalty cuts off any possibility of interconnection. Further, because hyper-loyalty is serving a similar emotional signaling role as anger, it is easy for the two to become intertwined. For example, I believe that I am showing the right level of loyalty to my group, and that my group will not mistake my level of commitment to our cause, when I express my loyalty by displaying anger towards outsiders or by publicly chastising a movement colleague who I feel is not sufficiently committed. My anger, which is motivated by hyper-loyalty, has a goal of knocking someone else down in order to raise myself up. In Nussbaum's terms, it is anger with a payback wish.

---

4. *Id.* at 6.

The hyper-loyalty dynamic has become even more pronounced in current times. The consequences of hyper-loyalty show up in the ways that activists articulate movement goals, in the ways that activists describe themselves and others, and in the ways that activists act. Activist Maurice Mitchell describes that dynamic as "maximalism." As Mitchell articulates, maximalism is "considering anything less than the most idealistic position as a betrayal of core values and evidence of corruption, cowardice, lack or commitment, or vision . . . [as well as] a righteous refusal to engage with people who do not already share our views and values."[5] Maximalism's expectation that every decision and every action be performed in its most ardent form means that activists repeatedly and regularly practice only one form of emotion—the emotion in its hot form. In other words, the appropriate way to demonstrate either one's approval of, and connection to another, or one's disapproval of, and distance from, another, is through an ardent expression of emotion. If I want to demonstrate my connection, I act with a maximal display of approval (i.e., love). If I want to demonstrate my disconnection, I act with a maximal display of disapproval (i.e., anger). Hyper-loyalty and maximalism overclaim certain kinds of interconnectedness and under-acknowledge other kinds.

There is a clear tension between our current social movement rules that prioritize hyper-loyalty and the idea of radical relationality. That tension seems intractable. Yet, the fact of interconnection itself may offer a way forward. As I noted earlier in the discussion about the moral value of anger, we use anger as a way of calling out injustice. Often, the injustice involves dignitary harm—the actions of one group cause harm to dignity interests of another group. We protest because we believe that a just society would equitably value every mem-

---

5. Maurice Mitchell, *Building Resilient Organizations*, THE FORGE (November 29, 2022), https://forgeorganizing.org/article/building-resilient -organizations.

ber's dignity. In other words, dignity is not zero sum. Dignity is not enhanced if it comes at the expense of another. The commitment to dignity for all is fundamentally based on the idea of radical relationality. My dignitary interests are tied to your interests, and our interests are tied to the dignitary interests of everyone else. While I surely may have a sense of my own individualized dignity, whether my dignity is being respected always has a relational component—respected by whom and as compared to whom?

Further, acknowledging the necessary fact of interconnection may help remind us that interconnection exists regardless of its valence. In other words, there is interconnectedness regardless of whether the relationality is positive, negative, or neutral. But our current practices of hyper-loyalty and maximalism encourage us to falsely believe that we have control over relationality. We mistakenly associate relationality only with positive connections. We mistakenly say that we have no kind of relationship with those with whom we disagree. We fail to acknowledge that the very fact of distancing or disconnecting from one another is a kind of relationality. Further, we presume that our practices of disconnection actually serve our desire for social change. We need to more rigorously inquire whether that presumption is accurate. Why would maximizing difference create social change? Similarly, we need to better understand why embracing relationality might be better at creating social change.

Critically, as we think about radical relationality and social change, it is not enough to say, "look forward, don't get stuck in the past." The past created the injustices and dignitary harm. The past is where we learned, or had imposed upon us, socially constructed rules about relationality—who is in this group or that group, what group has power, and the like. Thus, if radical relationality is to be useful, it cannot be understood as a call to forget the past—to love one's neighbor regardless of the neighbor's bad prior conduct. Radical relationality has to provide a mechanism for acknowledging past harm, and for ensuring accountability for future behavior.

This is the point where it is helpful to return to faith traditions. In particular, I want to explore an approach created by some U.S.-based, Buddhist theologians of color called "radical dharma."[6] As I noted earlier, a core concept in Buddhism is the idea that as a matter of descriptive fact, all living beings are interconnected. None of us escapes relationality, and none of us can entirely control the valence of relationality. We all can experience relationships that are positive and dignity enhancing, and we all can experience relationships that are negative and dignity denying. Buddhism further assesses that because we misperceive ourselves as independent from each other, that causes us to mistakenly believe that we can control relationality. As a result, we then act in ways that disregard interconnectedness, which in turn can cause us to act in ways that do not enhance the dignity of others. Contemporary Buddhist scholars have particularly explored how the disregard of interconnectedness foments both individual practices of unjust treatment and subordination as well as supports systems of unearned power and privilege.

Radical dharma brings a clear-eyed understanding of historical patterns of unjust relationality—both as between individuals and systemically. More pointedly, radical dharma requires that each of us understand histories of unjust relationships, such as slavery and other, more contemporary forms of subordination, and understand how those histories create and maintain overt and covert systems of subordination. From those historical lessons, radical dharma teaches that interconnectedness cannot be truly understood or experienced until those who have benefitted from unjust systems of subordination affirmatively act to dismantle those

---

6. "Dharma" is a Sanskrit word typically understood by Buddhists as referring to core teachings or lessons.

systems. Importantly, radical dharma requires mutuality of respect. It confronts Buddhist community members who have benefitted from systems of privilege and inquires what actions those members must take to be in right relationality with members of the community who have been denigrated by systems of privilege. It makes visible for community members who have experienced subordination how to ensure that Buddhist practices are not used to create a "kinder, gentler, suffering" that maintains "the unwholesome roots of systemic suffering . . ."[7]

Radical dharma is particular as well about the intentions that a community member should cultivate to support right relational actions. It rejects a mindset of largess—a white community member thinking "I am doing something for" community members of color—because that mindset maintains unearned power and privilege. Mutual relationality requires a different intent. It requires that each individual engage in their own practices for their own enlightenment because true enlightenment comes from understanding that every person carries some kind of burden created by systems of subordination. As Reverend angel Kyodo williams explains, whether a person is a community member with unearned privilege or a community member who experiences subordination, both persons get "policed" to ensure that systems of power remain in place.[8] The person with privilege who has a mindset of "doing something for" community members of color is both acceding to being policed (e.g., agreeing not to reject unearned privilege) and continuing to police (e.g., continuing to subordinate another by placing them in an inferior position). Radical dharma presses Buddhist practi-

---

7. Rev. angel Kyodo williams, *Introduction: Enter Here Radical Challenge, in* RADICAL DHARMA: TALKING RACE, LOVE AND LIBERATION xxiii (Rev. angel Kyodo williams, Lama Rod Owens & Jasmine Syedullah eds., 2016).
8. *Id.* at xxvii.

tioners—particularly members of the dominant white community—to move beyond a "hyper-individualized salvation model" to a genuine commitment to liberation for all living beings.[9]

Radical dharma shares a lineage of thought with other faith-based activist traditions like Martin Luther King, Jr.'s articulation of the Christian concept of *agape* love noted earlier. Dr. King, too, insisted on the fact of interconnectedness and on a moral requirement for a particular intention for the work of social change. In Dr. King's framing, the goal was to move toward a "beloved community" and achieving that required love in action. As Dr. King said:

> . . . I am cognizant of the interrelatedness of all communities and states. I cannot sit idly by in Atlanta and not be concerned about what happens in Birmingham. Injustice anywhere is a threat to justice everywhere. We are caught in an inescapable network of mutuality, tied in a single garment of destiny.[10]

In the face of segregation and Jim Crow, that inescapable mutuality necessarily created tension, and Dr. King saw such tension as constructive if met with nonviolent resistance. Nonviolent resistance was love in action. Its goal was to dismantle unjust systems to then build a shared, mutual, beloved community.

I think radical dharma and similar practices like love in action help us as activists see that acknowledging the fact of interconnectedness is not the same as accepting the status quo or failing to honor the past or capitulating to those in power. To accept that relationality is inherently and necessarily some-

---

9. *Id.* at xxv.
10. Martin Luther King, Jr., *Letter From Birmingham Jail, in* A Testament of Hope: The Essential Writings and Speeches of Martin Luther King, Jr. 290 (James M. Washington ed., 1968).

thing that comes with being alive in a world full of others just is to acknowledge a fact of the world. Acknowledging that fact is nothing more than acknowledging a fact. What we each do as a result of that knowledge is a separate matter.

Radical dharma proposes meeting relationality with the practice of fierce love. Our first thought about fierce love may be to think it means something like hyper-loyalty. To be fierce about my relationships might mean to be ardent and to defend them against all challenges. I might think that I need to show fierce love to protect my relationships because there are others trying to break down the solidarity within my community. Radical dharma understands fierce love differently. Fierceness does not equate with loyalty, but instead with a willingness to pause and create space to investigate and acknowledge the contours of any particular relationship or web of relationships. In other words, instead of presuming that a specific kind of relationship requires me to act in certain ways, I pause and reflect on the relationship as fully and with as clear eyes as I am able. The reflective pause is fierce because it demands that I push myself to see beyond my assumptions about a relationship (i.e., that it is positive or negative), and to see beyond the accepted, and socially constructed, emotional labor rules about the relationship. It is fierce because it is unflinching about fully seeing societal conditions and constructions about a relationship (i.e., that the relationship may reflect an unjust power hierarchy).

For example, as an activist, taking a reflective pause to inquire about the relationality with my movement colleagues, I may see patterns that I had not attended to before because I thought the right way to act within the movement was to demonstrate hyper-loyalty. My reflective pause may show me ways that my own acts of hyper-loyalty shut down participation by my colleagues, just as the pause may also show me ways that my acts of loyalty help newcomers feel welcomed into movement work. Fierce love is fierce because it requires me to be purposeful in my reflections, and to understand that my own perceptions are partial. I can only know my own experience of any particular relationship. Fierce love reminds me that because my own perceptions are partial, I have a responsibility to learn what I am missing. How are my actions experienced by others? What feeling and framing rules am I bringing to a relationship and are those the same as others involved? Have I categorized some kinds of relationships inaccurately, and in ways that have led me to disengage instead of engaging?

Taking a reflective pause is a starting practice that is intended to lead into a longer, more sustained set of contemplative efforts. For Buddhists, the reflective pause is not transformative in and of itself, but is situated within a larger set of practices that together, and over time, are intended to be transformative. However, I think the pause is useful precisely because it is a small and readily achievable interruption to our well-practiced habits. As I have noted, as activists, we believe our actions of hyper-loyalty are useful, and we are firmly committed to those practices. We will not set those aside easily, and we surely will be skeptical of any promise of a magic bullet. The reflective pause asks us to start gently—to accept that my experiences are not universal, and to ask simply "what am I missing from my perspective right now?"

That simple starting point of asking "what am I missing" is crucial, I think, because it sets up the possibility of many answers, not one "right" answer. Being open to multiple answers includes both the possibility that I have assessed the situation accurately, and the possibility that I have missed something important. The reflective pause does not ask me to unilaterally jettison emotion rules and practices that may have value. The pause asks me only to make sure that I am making a wise choice in the moment, given the information I have. It also sets me up to be open to changing that choice at later decision-making moments as I learn more.

What follows, then, from a reflective pause? As I noted, the reflective pause is a starting point, and traditions like fierce love or love in action have a larger goal of transforming our society into a just place for all. This is the point where I think it is helpful to return to our conversation about quietude and the ways in which cultivating an expansive, open, and inquiring internal life can lay the foundation for transformative change. When we considered the idea of "listening for God" as a revelatory practice, I reflected on how an open mindset could be particularly useful when faced with seemingly intractable issues. When I have a curious mindset with no expectation about what I will hear when I listen, I am better able both to hear something new and unexpected, as well as to hear something different within information that I already know. Building on the practice of a reflective pause, and the larger commitment to quietude as a way of manifesting resistance, fierce love helps me to disrupt my habits of viewing things partially. To then move from a clearer-eyed perspective to transformative action, I need to develop my capacity to be open to the unexpected. Here, again, faith traditions can offer a useful idea—that of abiding love.

Like the concept of "love of neighbor," the idea of "abiding love" is more nuanced than it may seem at first consideration. We often think of "abide" as another way of saying "obey" or "comply." I am supposed to abide by the law. Or, in a more direct context for us, I abide by feeling and framing rules about emotional labor. Faith traditions certainly include that sense of the word. For example, in the New Testament, the Book of John offers the following lesson: "If ye keep my commandments, ye shall abide in my love; even as I have kept my Father's commandments, and abide in his love."[11] But, there is a more expansive sense of "abide," both as a matter of definition and as a matter of religious teachings. In addition to obey, abide

---

11. *John* 15:10 (King James Version).

can mean a physical place of residing—"I abide in this town." It also can mean to stand steady or at the ready—"I abide my time until they change their minds."

Faith traditions harness the more expansive meanings of abide. Particularly for Christian traditions, abide is a sense of standing steady with another (often God), in readiness to learn and understand. Further, abiding love is constant. It calls on me to maintain my relationship with another even when the other acts in ways in which I disagree. In other words, abiding love has the same recognition of, and commitment to, the interconnectedness between all of us. To show abiding love is to understand that relationality does not disappear just because someone acts badly towards me. I think it is helpful here to check ourselves about the word "love," and to remind ourselves of Dr. King's teaching about the differences between *eros, philia,* and *agape*.[12] Abiding love is based on *agape*, not on other ideas of love. Thus, abiding love brings the same viewpoint to relationality as does fierce love. Abiding love does not require me to agree with, or apologize for, wrongful behavior of another. It does, however, call on me to stand steady in relationship with others, to make my own efforts to develop a more just relationship, and to take actions that prompt others to change their behaviors as well.

Buddhism offers a congruent set of teachings that may provide another useful perspective. Particularly in Mahayana schools of Buddhism, the concept of "abiding" is rooted the ideas of being situated in a place or remaining in a space. Buddhism conceives of place and space not as physical locations, but as states of mind. I can have an abiding mind in several different ways. If I cannot get something out of my head, such as a narrative that keeps running through my

---

12. Martin Luther King, Jr., *Facing the Challenge of a New Age,* in A Testament of Hope: The Essential Writings and Speeches of Martin Luther King, Jr. 135 (James M. Washington, ed. 1968).

mind about an interaction I had with a work colleague, I am abiding on that narrative. For Buddhism, that kind of habituated clinging to a narrative is considered unhelpful and unproductive. I also could intentionally choose to focus my awareness on a particular item in order to practice concentration. My concentration practice is designed to help me fully see something (tangible or intangible) instead of looking at the object in a more habituated way. For example, if I am looking at a tangible object, like a flower, I don't let my mind say "flower" and move on to a story in my head about why I like flowers and how it makes me happy when someone gives me them. Instead, I focus my mind on the particular flower in front of me. I consider each petal and notice changes in shape and color. I try and discern smells and textures. I work at holding my mind on this flower in this moment, and I try not to let my mind wander off. Buddhism thinks positively of that kind of abiding concentration because it interrupts the brain's chatter. It also affirms the teaching of constant change—not only because I may see differences in the flower during my concentration practice, but also because I know that I would see differences even if I came back to the flower at the end of the day.

Buddhism has a related mindfulness practice called abiding in stillness, also known as non-abiding. Instead of focusing on a particular object, my practice is to have my mind attend as fulling as possible to every piece of information coming to my senses. I notice how the ambient air temperature feels on my skin and the differences between my uncovered and clothed skin. I notice all of the small sounds that my ears take in—whether the hum of a fan or a bird chirping or my own breathing. The practice of non-abiding also interrupts my mind's chatter. If my mind wanders, I bring it back to open awareness. The practice develops my capacity to see the interconnectedness of all things, and to be aware of the fact that the only stable truth is that there is constant change.

For Buddhism, the abiding practices are intended to be re-velatory, although in a different way than being given divine knowledge as with Abrahamic traditions. The abiding practic-es reveal the descriptive facts of interconnectedness and con-stant change. Buddhism teaches that when we struggle against those facts by clinging to a false idea that we are separate from everyone else and that we can keep things constant, we com-mit ourselves to lives that always feel akimbo and fail to fully flourish. Instead, when we embrace interconnectedness and constant change, we can cultivate equanimity, compassion, and lovingkindness. In other words, we have abiding love for all those around us. We build our capacity to have an open, inquiring mind—one that can see justice and injustice, while also recognizing interconnectedness.

Let me return, then, to the question I posed earlier about whether embracing the kind of clear-eyed relationality called for by both fierce and abiding love might better set up the pos-sibility of social change than does embracing disconnection, or "us/them" relationality. I believe that it does—pragmatical-ly and normatively.

Pragmatically, to change something across society ulti-mately requires changing the behavior of a large number of people. Embracing connection helps remind me that each person holds the potential to become a participant in social change. Acknowledging the fact of interconnection helps me resist inaccurately categorizing a person as an "enemy" from the start. To acknowledge interconnection is not to be naïve about relationships. There will be people who are uninterest-ed in social change and who actively desire to maintain the status quo. Seeing interconnection is not enough, in and of itself. But it fosters a mindset that encourages me to continue forward. Normatively, embracing interconnection requires me to let go of a payback wish. It requires me to attend to past conduct, but to direct my actions forward in ways that enhance dignity across all relationships. For change to genuinely transform society, instead of just replacing one set of discriminating factors for another, the change must enhance dignity for all and create conditions for everyone to have the capacity to lead a flourishing life.

Importantly, transformative change requires more than a mindset. It requires action. The actions that are called for by embracing interconnection may be different depending on how I find myself currently situated. For example, if I am a member of dominant society, I must see and understand both the obvious and the hidden ways in which I have received benefits or privileges at the expense of others. I must be able to assess on what basis I have been given those benefits or privileges—be it effort, luck, race, gender, or other reasons. I need to assess which of those reasons support a just world, and which do not. I also need to be able to see beyond individual actions so that I can identify systems and structures that support unjust benefits and privileges. Further, I must understand that setting down my unearned benefits and privileges is not altruistic—I am not doing something for another. Instead, setting down unearned privileges is the way for me to engage with others so that our relationships genuinely enhance mutual dignity. As a person experiencing privilege, I have a responsibility to take affirmative actions that demonstrate to those who have been unfairly denied benefits and privilege that I am committed to creating a "beloved community," to use Dr. King's framing. I cannot expect others to trust me without me first earning such trust through my own conduct.

If I have been disempowered, I can acknowledge interconnectedness with nuance. Among those whom I experience as part of my group and for whom I readily feel connection, I can take actions that affirm that safe space of insiders. At the same time, I need to resist actions within my group that reinforce hyper-loyalty. I also can resist maximizing differences—both differences within my own group and differences across other groups where allyship might be fostered. With those whom I experience as benefiting from the dominant society, I can see connection with open, welcoming skepticism. I can stand ready to observe actions from another to confirm that there is a positive relationship that can be fostered. I do not have to trust a relationship before there are actions that prove such trust is warranted, but I should be wary of a mindset that unilaterally writes off the possibility of connection.

For everyone, embracing interconnection requires an ability to foster accountability with compassion. None of us will be perfect at maintaining right relationality all of the time. All of us will misstep, and treat someone poorly. All of us may be treated poorly by another. In those moments where we misstep, I think we are most prone to relying on unhelpful habits, particularly habits about emotional labor. As we investigated earlier when considering anger in social movement work, we prioritize feeling and framing rules that call on us to respond maximally. We express anger in its hot form, and in ways that break connections. We chastise each other as disloyal for emotional expressions that are less than hot. In that punitive form, anger masquerades as accountability. Once I am able to recognize the actual fact that I will misstep at some point, I can acknowledge my hope that my misstep will be met with compassion. That lets me see alternative ways that I can ask another to be accountable for their mistake. I do not need to respond maximally. Even if the misstep is one that would justify my apt anger, I have a choice in how I ask the wrongdoer to be accountable for their actions. I can do so in ways that seek to maintain a connection, while still being clear with the wrongdoer that they do not get a pass for their bad actions. Compassion does not mean quiet acceptance. To harken back to the teaching of Reverend angel Kyodo williams, compassion is a not a kinder, gentler form of suffering.

Up to now, I have been talking about interconnectedness in more general terms. As we have noted, interconnectedness can include positive, neutral, or negative relationships. Relationships also can have a range of purposes. For example, in social movement work, activists often think that we are in relationship with others in our movement because we have the same view about what are the key requirements for a good and just society. In other words, we base our sense of interconnection on an assumption about shared ideology. And we base disconnection on perceptions about how the ideologies of others do not match our own at all, or that even if the broader ideologies between two groups are similar, that my group prioritizes a different set of more specific values than does another group. I then describe connections across groups as positive, negative, or neutral primarily based on whether I assess that the specific ideological commitments of my group either line up with, are not considered by, or are ranked as less important by, another group. This practice is a sibling to hyper-loyalty. I require a precision in how another group's worldviews and priorities match up with mine before I will collaborate. To do otherwise would require me to be less than hyper-loyal to my own group. I do not notice that my choices reinforce fragmentation among people seeking social change. If I am right about my pragmatic point that social change happens most often, and most effectively, when many people come together, then keeping groups fragmented serves to maintain the status quo.

Building the capacity to compassionately ask others to be accountable for their actions is one way to disrupt our habits of disconnection and to create an ability to acknowledge that interconnection exists regardless of how closely we share ideological commitments. When we trust that we have the capacity and skillfulness to work together with mutual respect, that allows us to set down our habit of presuming disconnection. Further, we can begin to build connections by finding ways to mutually support each other that do not require our movement groups to have the exact same priorities. For example, my group may have extra supplies that another group could use for its next community meeting. Another group may have reserved space at a community event and could share its table with my group. Groups working within the same community could come together to help launch a free grocery store in the neighborhood.

That idea of mutual aid in terms of supporting basic needs is not new, and there is a long history of activists coming together across movements to help meet needs in their communities. Scholar and activist Dean Spade describes mutual aid in this straightforward way: "Mutual aid is collective coordination to meet each other's needs. . . ."[13] One well-known mutual aid program in the U.S. was the free breakfast program created by the Black Panther Party to feed children in Oakland, California. At the time, there were no state or federally funded free breakfast programs for school children in the Bay Area. The Black Panther Party did not require that families participate in the Party's social movement work in order to qualify for the free meals. The meals were a direct response to a basic need in the community. The core commitment behind mutual aid is that solidarity is built through reciprocity, not charity or largess. It is consonant with the practice of radical dharma that right relationality requires us to account for ourselves and our own practices, and to reject the idea of "doing something *for*" another. Importantly, mutual aid focuses first on fundamental needs, not ideology. Participating in mutual aid gives me a way to do something *with* another, without us first having to make sure that our ideological commitments perfectly line up.

As we work together, it is likely that I will discover other commonalities I have with the people with whom I am engaging. Dean Spade describes participating in mutual aid at

---

13. Dean Spade, MUTUAL AID: BUILDING SOLIDARITY DURING THIS CRISIS (AND THE NEXT) 7 (2020).

the Sylvia Rivera Law Project in New York. The Project offers free legal help to people who identify as trans or gender-nonconforming. While people shared the need for legal aid, their problems crossed many different systems, including housing, healthcare, immigration. The Project invited people to join together in various educational programs, regardless of ideology. As Spade notes, "things were often bumpy," but coming together over the mutual need for legal aid gave folks ways to "learn about experiences different from theirs and built solidarity across those differences."[14]

If we think about mutual aid through our frame of interconnectedness, mutual aid is an approach that begins by finding a ready connection between people—their shared need for a core service or good—and uses that connection as the doorway through which people enter, and then can discover the deeper, inextricable interconnectedness between themselves and all others. Like fierce love or abiding love, mutual aid is both action and mindset. It takes descriptive facts in a society—there are people who do not have reliable access to food; there are people who do not have reliable employment—and uses those facts to mobilize community members to take actions to support one another because they understand that the needs are shared by all. Each of us can enhance our own dignity by enhancing the dignity of those with whom we are connected. As Dean Spade has observed: "Solidarity across issues and populations is what makes movements big and powerful. Without that connection, we end up with disconnected groups, working in their issue silos, undermining each other, competing for attention and funding, not backing each other up and not building power."[15]

I started this chapter describing some of the current social constructions of "love" within activist groups, and the ways

---

14. *Id.* at 14.
15. *Id.* at 15.

in which rules about emotional labor push activists to see expanding relationships with others as threatening instead of as connecting. I think it is critical to understand and acknowledge that activists who are working to unsettle the status quo have lived experiences that reasonably cause them to be cautious about who they trust. I have tried to illustrate that the challenging dynamic, however, is that we practice distrust so often that we have neglected to build our capacity to see connections. I have offered some alternatives, including fierce and abiding love and mutual aid, with the goal of reminding, re-expanding, and re-engaging our ability to experience mutual relationality. And, we have continued to explore some key benefits of mutual relationality and social movement work—how it can bring more people into shared endeavors for change and how it can catalyze new perspectives on strategies and actions.

Throughout our conversations in this book, I have noted moments about social change work and the law. Now that we have some shared foundations about emotional labor rules in social movement work and their positive and challenging consequences, we can layer on a more thorough investigation of whether and how the law matters. The next chapter takes up that inquiry.

5

The Role of Law

UP TO THIS POINT, WE HAVE BEEN FOCUSED on the interplay between social movement work, emotions, and rules about emotions and activism. We have seen how the emotions of anger and love prevail in activist work, and that both often get simplified and amplified into their most ardent forms. We have thought about when those "hot" forms of anger and love serve activists well, and how they also impinge activists, limiting perspectives and limiting alliances. We have considered what might be gained if we cultivated the capacity for radical relationality, seeing both the hopefulness of mutuality, and the challenges of finding genuine mutuality in a society steeped in power, control, and histories of subordination.

Throughout, I have given some examples of how people, especially those who hold political power, use the law to perpetuate emotional rules that help maintain power and control. In this chapter, I want to investigate more particularly how "the law" plays a role in building and constraining relationality and what that might mean for activists. When activists assess whether they should be hopeful or skeptical about using the law to catalyze social change, is it useful for activists to pay specific attention to the way the law orders relationality? I will suggest that because "the law" is made by people in power, it typically preserves the status quo in some fundamental ways. If the change that is desired is notable, it will take a great number of people in support in order to disrupt those in power and push through the desired change. Thus, it may be that it matters less whether we are hopeful or skeptical about the law, and it may matter more whether we have built productive and transformative practices about relationality.

To lay some groundwork, I want to first frame how we might more overtly think about the law in relational terms. In our everyday lives, we often speak about "the law" as if it is an independent thing. The law says that I should stop my car at a red light. The law tells me whether I can build a porch onto my manufactured home. The law tells my employer what is the minimum hourly wage that I must be paid. While all of us know that the law is made by people, we have habits of thought that subtly push the people to the periphery. That causes us to think about the law as relational mostly in the sense that there is a relationship between "the law" and the people whose behavior the law targets. The law becomes disembodied. In other words, we start to detach "the law" from the people who make it. That then may cause us to think about a dynamic of social change that gets described as: "Changing the law is the way we change society." When we give "the law" its own independence, we obscure the more accurate description of law's relationality—that one group of people have power to set out rules that will control not only their behavior, but also the behavior of a much larger group of people.

Further, when we frame the law as something that stands on its own, we tacitly imply that the law has some special capacity to change the ways in which people stand in relationship with each other. Or, to put it another way, when we treat the law as its own independent thing, and say that the law can change how society works, we are suggesting that the law is imbued with some special capacity to change the way people view each other. If we take a moment to consider that proposition, especially thinking about our own lived experiences as social activists, I think many of us will readily acknowledge that "the law" has no *special* capacity to change people's views. The law may have the capacity to cram down certain behaviors on people, or restrict their behaviors, but mandating behavior does not necessarily nor ineluctably change mindsets. As activists, we may worry that begrudgingly changing behavior does not get us to our genuine end goal of a just society.

There is a rich body of literature—both empirical and philosophical—that has investigated when, how, and what role the law plays in catalyzing social change. For example, scholars have studied how taking a dispute to court may or may not lead to social change. Consider the important and well-known U.S. Supreme Court decision, *Brown v. Board of Education*, where scholars have investigated and tested the popularized notion that *Brown* ended school segregation.[1] Similarly, scholars have looked at the range of advocacy methods available to activists and compared and contrasted methods for efficacy and accessibility. For example, activists can choose between advocacy methods such as organizing, litigating, legislative or regulatory advocacy, among others. There is much to be gained by understanding what contextual factors set up one advocacy method to lead to better results than another and what factors make an advocacy method more or less accessible to activists at any given time. As activists, I would encourage us to delve into the manifold resources already available that help us build our knowledge about how to best choose

---

1. *See generally* SHADES OF BROWN: NEW PERSPECTIVES ON SCHOOL DESEGREGATION (Derrick Bell ed., 1980).

advocacy methods and how to see with more nuance the impact of legal changes through the courts or legislatures.

My endeavor here is different. I want to focus on the relationality that always is embedded in the law. I want to foreground the people, and by doing so to better understand what kind of relationality is being created, prohibited, or controlled by a law and for what purpose. For example, some laws appear to focus facially on individual relationships—think about family law and the way it orders the lives of people who marry each other or who have children together. Or think about personal injury law and the way that it allocates blame for a harm that happens mostly between individuals—like who has to pay money to whom after an accident. Other laws set up standards that are supposed to apply equivalently to an entire community and are presented as benefiting the community equally. Think about building codes that list the kinds of safe construction materials that can be used in residential homes. Or noise ordinances that provide for quiet hours across a community. Finally, there are laws where the relational focus is on supporting association among people. Think here about laws that create entities like membership associations or that foster associations among people engaged in the same endeavor, like labor unions.

There are no bright lines between different kinds of law and relationality. A law that sets up standards for a community also impacts individual relationships within that community. If I am your neighbor and you call the police because I won't turn down my music late at night, that affects our individual relationship as much as the law's effort to set out a community standard. And laws about individual relationships can be a tool to enforce systematic, community-wide norms—both discriminatory and equitable. Think about laws that prohibited same-sex or interracial couples from marrying, and the changes to those laws. I think that exploring how a law orders relationality from multiple perspectives may help us, as social activists, uncover some interesting information that relates to the conversations we have been having about emotions, relationality, and activism.

First, how we perceive the relationality of a law may influence what we choose as the emotional feeling and framing rules we most likely deploy. For example, if we think about a law as ordering relationships between individuals, that may dispose us to think that the purpose of the law is to tell two people how they are supposed to behave towards each other. The tort law of battery tells me that I am not supposed to hit another person, and that if I do, the law could be used to make me atone in some way. The law also tells the person I hit that they are entitled to feel wronged. And, if a person has been wronged, we have feeling and framing rules that support the person feeling and showing anger. The law also signals to the person who has been wronged that they can seek payback in certain ways. In other words, the law permits the wronged person to have me give up something, often money, in order to rectify my bad conduct. The legal norms behind tort law do not describe the system as about payback. Instead, tort law is described as a system for justly allocating responsibility for harm. But, for the individuals involved, the experience and emotions likely follow more ordinary feeling and framing rules. I imbue the law with motivations that are tied to the emotions I experience when encountering the law. For me, tort law is designed to assign blame and make someone responsible for redressing the wrong.

But the very same experience may prompt different emotions depending on a person's lived experiences. Take tort law again, but a different example than one person intentionally hitting another—torts that relate to personal privacy. The generally articulated goal of privacy torts is that an individual has the right to keep some kinds of information private. For example, one privacy tort, known as the disclosure tort, says that you have a right to sue me if I publicly disclose private information about you without your permission. If, without permission, I announced to a large crowd that you had received medical treatment for a sensitive health issue, the disclosure tort permits you to sue me for the harm I caused. When the experience is framed in that way, it may seem similar to my example of one person hitting another. I hurt you; you are entitled to be angry and to seek payback from me.

Let me change the hypothetical above slightly. The disclosure that I made about you related to a medical condition that is not experienced by everyone. I revealed publicly that you are a woman who has been unable to conceive a child. You may feel harmed not only individually, but also because of gendered societal expectations about what it means to be a woman. Part of the harm you experience relates to social constructions about what it means to be a "woman" and what the dominant society requires of women—that they bear children. The harm you experience is personal, because I have slighted you. The harm you experience is larger and more categorical because society has harmed you with its unfair gender expectations. The anger you feel is not just personal, but also is an expression of injustice. It is the kind of apt anger we considered earlier.

Legal scholars like Martha Chamallas and Scott Skinner-Thompson, among others, have written eloquently about the ways in which tort law fails to acknowledge or address those larger, structural harms. For example, Chamallas has demonstrated how the way in which tort law translates "harm" into a dollar amount for an award of damages includes rules that devalue particular kinds of effort that women most often undertake (like work within the household) and rules that devalue how women may report that they experience harm (like emotional distress).[2] Similarly, Skinner-Thompson has

---

2. *See* Martha Chamallas, *The Architecture of Bias: Deep Structures in Tort Law*, 146 U. PA. L. REV. 463 (1998); *Civil Rights in Ordinary Tort Cases: Race,*

evaluated how the law about privacy torts, like the disclosure tort in the example above, have been applied in categorically inequitable ways. In particular, he has demonstrated how courts scrutinize privacy tort claims more favorably for plaintiffs who hold privileged positions in society than those who do not (like outed LGBTQ plaintiffs).[3] Chamallas and Skinner-Thompson describe how tort law does not have overt and explicit doctrine that requires tort law to ignore the ways in which societal norms systematically impact how tort law is applied to different groups. Instead, those societal norms creep into tort law and their impacts often are ignored.

As a system, tort law tethers itself to the idea of individualized harm. Even in situations of "mass" torts, like harm caused to many members of a community when a manufacturing plant dumps toxic waste, tort law asks what harm each individual experienced from being exposed to toxic waste. Tort law privileges individual relational connections. It encourages us to focus on one person's behavior, and it sets up feeling and framing rules related to that individual. Tort law encourages me to see the other person as an adversary instead of someone with whom I might have common ground. As a result, it is easier for me to choose feeling and framing rules, like anger with a payback wish, because tort law says I succeed only if I can effectively place blame on another. The structure of tort law is a mechanism for building distance between people instead of connection. It fractures relationality. Or, to put it another way, it builds negative relationality.

The dynamic of tort law is interesting because it demonstrates how the law orchestrates how we experience the inescapable fact of relationality, and often does so in obscured ways. There is no explicit doctrine in tort law that says that a goal of

Gender, and the Calculation of Economic Loss, 38 Loy. L.A. L. Rev. 133 (1982).

3. See Scott Skinner-Thompson, Privacy's Double Standard, 93 Wash. L. Rev. 2051 (2018).

tort law is to make people see each other as adversaries. But that is what happens. That is important knowledge because, as social activists, if social change requires the support of many community members, and not just a small group, we need to find ways for community members to see themselves in solidarity with each other, and not as adversaries.

What I think is particularly important about the work of scholars like Chamallas and Skinner-Thompson is how it reveals that tort law is not only about relationality between individuals. When we look at tort law more carefully, we can see that it is deeply infused with relationality across communities and groups. Further, that relationality is dynamic—it is positive, negative, and neutral, and those valences can travel in multiple directions across the web of relationality. Once that web of relationality is revealed, we can see how what appeared to be individual harms are harms to a web of relationships. If, as a woman, the damages I will receive for lost economic activity are less than those awarded to a similarly situated man, I am personally harmed *and* I am harmed as a member of a larger group in society. Recognizing the web of relationality expands the possibilities for the kinds of emotional labor that I may find appropriate. Instead of focusing on feeling and framing rules about individual relationships and directing my emotional response toward one person, I step back and think about a collective response. Once I do that, I am more likely to see structural harms and to consider collective injustices. I find common ground with others, not just adversarialness.

I find common ground in part because I realize that a law that appears to be about individual relationships also can be mobilized against groups. That helps me recognize a different way that I may be vulnerable to the law—not only as an individual, but also as a group member. In turn, that may help me see some possibilities of solidarity where I had missed those connections before. Philosopher Myisha Cherry has labeled that kind of relationality "vulnerable solidarity."[4] Cherry explores how connecting the idea of being vulnerable to the law with the recognition of interconnectedness between people helps build solidarity—particularly as it relates to changing society through changing the law. Cherry more broadly frames change through the lens of democratic action, but democratic action includes changes in "the state" (to use Cherry's term), which then lead to changes in the law. As Cherry describes it:

> Vulnerable solidarity is solidarity that is formed based on the vulnerability that we all face as citizens to be targeted and/or affected by state racism and state violence. . . . In vulnerable solidarity, citizens understand that we all are susceptible to attack or harm by the state. . . . Instead of joining a cause because it has a direct impact on our social positioning now, people will join causes because they will know that all injustices have an impact on us all; if not directly, indirectly, if not now, in the future.[5]

As I noted, seeing how the law can create collective harm can help reposition my choices about the kind of emotional work that best leads to broad social change. Seeing that I am not the only one at risk for an unjust result under the law can help me transform my anger from the kind that includes a payback wish to apt anger that seeks forward-looking change to improve results for everyone. As Cherry frames it, what once mistakenly looked like individualized vulnerability gets more accurately understood as a risk of harm shared by everyone. When we put people and webs of relationships back into "the law," that also reminds us that the law is human made, and that we hold the potential to change it. We

---

4. Myisha Cherry, *State Racism, State Violence, and Vulnerable Solidarity*, in THE OXFORD HANDBOOK OF PHILOSOPHY AND RACE 352–62 (Naomi Zack ed., 2017).

5. *Id.* at 360–61.

are reminded that finding and building connections across people is the way people come together in sufficient numbers to change the institutions that make law (at least in a democratic society). Cherry captures that idea succinctly when she says: "Democracy is . . . about the people's relationship with each other."[6]

Cherry's idea of vulnerable solidarity sits nicely alongside the idea of mutual aid we considered in the last chapter. Both frames encourage us to see the positive possibilities of relationality instead of the negative. Whether it is that we acknowledge that all of us are harmed by injustice or we acknowledge that all of us have basic needs, we can see connections where we might otherwise have focused on differences. As social activists, if one of our strategies for change includes adjusting "the law," then we may need to start by reframing the prevalent narrative about that law. For example, one of the narrative changes that supporters of same-sex marriage pressed was that the issue was not about *who* could marry, but about respect for the social institution of marriage. When the narrative about same-sex marriage was framed individually (i.e., who can marry whom), then relationality was adversarial (i.e., I can marry, but you cannot). When the narrative about same-sex marriage was framed as about respecting marriage as an institution, then the relationality was more collective—marriage brings about good consequences in society, therefore the law should be used to encourage marriage across society. Building a relational narrative helps people see common ground. If people can see common ground among themselves, that can increase the number of people who will support changes in the law.

Within "the law" we can find existing examples of structures in support of community relationality. An example noted above that likely comes readily to mind are laws that

---

6. *Id.* at 360.

support labor organizing. On their face, laws about labor organizing are about protecting the ability of communities of workers to come together—both to create affiliation among workers, and to create a unified presence towards employers. At its best, labor law is intended to build a particular community—workers—for the purpose of redistributing the relational power between employers and employees so that employees have a say in their conditions of employment. As such, labor law encourages emotion feeling and framing rules that call for displays of connection, solidarity, and loyalty amongst workers. To be an effective workers' organization, members commit to the idea that the way for each of them to benefit individually is to create a set of collective benefits. Members commit to setting aside individualized strategies for strategies that lead to mutual gain.

Of course, labor law cannot be disembodied from the people holding the power to make law. Just like tort law has more covertly developed in ways that embed systemic discrimination into laws about personal injuries, labor law has developed in ways to mute its collective power. At times, the efforts to dismantle worker organizing have been overt, violent, and a clear display of power and control. For example, labor law scholar and historian Ahmed White, whose work was noted earlier, has carefully investigated and documented how capitalists with power crushed the International Workers of the World shortly after World War I in the United States.[7]

But there also have been subtler efforts, cloaked in rationales about a worker's individual autonomy and choice. For example, in 2018, the U.S. Supreme Court issued its ruling in *Janus v. AFSCME*.[8] That case involved a government employee who was protected under a collective bargaining agreement

---

7. Ahmed White, UNDER THE IRON HEEL: THE WOBBLIES AND THE CAPITALIST WAR ON RADICAL WORKERS (2022).

8. *Janus v. Amer. Federation of State, County & Municipal Employees Council*, 138 S. Ct. 2448 (2018).

between a union and the government employer. Even though the union's agreement benefited the employee, the employee did not want to join the union, and objected to paying dues to the union. The Supreme Court ruled that the employee's personal choice about the union was more important than the fact that the union's efforts (and expenditures) benefitted the employee through the collective bargaining agreement. The Court overruled its own longstanding precedent, which had permitted the employee to choose not to join the union, but required the employee to pay dues in order to compensate the union for its work. Couching its decision in terms of individual rights under the First Amendment, the Supreme Court changed its course and permitted the employee to refuse to pay dues to the union while continuing to benefit from the union's representation.

My point here is not one about the proper reach of the First Amendment in employment settings. People can reasonably disagree on how to best respect an individual's choice about not associating with a group, even if that group is benefitting the individual. That reasonable minds can disagree is proven by the fact that for almost 50 years the Supreme Court followed exactly the opposite rule than it announced in *Janus*, and had approved of government employees paying some dues to a union even if the employee chose not to fully join the union. My point is that labor law, which on its face is designed to build communities, can be astutely denuded. Just like tort law cannot be disembodied from the people who make it, labor law also cannot. The people who make the law that is supposedly about protecting and building community amongst workers have the power to mold what are the approved contours of such a "community" and when those contours are to be restrained.

One of the interesting consequences of laws that seek to structure communities is that they can prompt similar emotional labor rules like the ones we have been discussing related to social movements. In other words, there are feeling and framing rules that relate to being a part of a group (or being excluded from a group) that get applied to communities constructed by the law just like those rules get applied to communities constructed through social activism. Consider labor unions, where there are feeling and framing rules that expect union members to show hyper-loyalty to their union. Employers and nonunion members are adversaries and not to be trusted. At the same time, unions are important places of positive emotional labor. Similar to other social movements, union members experience solidarity and support not just about employment issues. Members may initially come together because they work similar jobs. But they can find deeper connections because their union work gives them time and space to get to know each other. They find common ground beyond the work conditions that they share. They find ways to support each other outside of work.

Observing the dynamics of emotional labor in labor unions not only reminds us that there can be competing feeling and framing rules that apply to the same setting, but also helps reveal how the law can be used to manipulate which rules are more likely to apply. Worker organizing, including through labor unions, has a goal of shifting and rebalancing power. At least in the United States where the idea of free markets and capitalism predominate, power is held by those with more resources. In the employment context, that means employers have more power, including the choice to cram down less beneficial employment conditions on employees. The law can be used to mitigate that dynamic, and labor law purportedly does so. But, as we have been noting throughout this chapter, labor law cannot be disentangled from the people who have the power to make it. If those people have a goal of protecting employers from too much disruption, then they can craft labor law in ways that subtly undermine its effectiveness. The Supreme Court's decision in *Janus v. AFSCME* is an apt illustration of that dynamic. While federal labor law statutes require an employer to negotiate with an employee-approved labor union, the union is undermined by the Court's decision to permit employees to opt out of financially supporting the union's efforts. Further, instead of employees finding common ground among themselves, the Court's framing of its ruling in terms of the First Amendment sends a message that employees are pitted against each other—it is my First Amendment right to join the union versus your First Amendment right to abstain from joining.

A critical point that I hope my illustrations above demonstrate is that we, the people affected by and engaged with the law, have choices about what kind of relationality we choose to foreground when we put law into action. For almost every kind of law, we can make choices that prioritize individual, adversarial relationality or choices that prioritize more collective, community-enhancing relationality. Those choices can dramatically impact our efforts to preserve or change the law. When we foreground adversarial relationality, we make individuals choose a side against other individuals. We frame the question as one about whose particular interest the law should protect as against another's interest that the law should treat as less important. The framing makes it seem like the only available outcome of the law is one that is zero sum. If you win, I lose, and vice versa.

We often try and justify a law in a way that tries to obscure adversarial relationality. For example, think about the tort law example above related to personal injuries. One justification we offer for tort law is that all members of society benefit by having one person pay another person money for being harmed because that sets up a system to encourage every individual to undertake actions with a reasonable level of care. Therefore, making a person pay for harm caused to another because the person did not use reasonable care is just a way of serving the broader goal of ensuring societal wellbeing. But the way we operationalize tort law is that we make one person sue another person. The disagreements are personal and individualized. When we constantly experience a law as about fights between individuals, we practice seeing disconnection not connection. That can make it hard to coalesce a broader group to support changing the law.

If we make a different choice, and we foreground interconnectedness in the law, we create a chance to change the dynamic. As the example about how to more equitably calculate economic damages between women and men, and the example about same-sex marriage as about respecting the overall societal benefits that come from marriage demonstrate, *we* make the choice about how to see law's relationality. The law does not make that choice for us. If a core component to changing the law is to amass enough people who believe the law should change, that is critical, strategic knowledge that can be harnessed by activists. As activists consider how they develop their strategy of change, it is beneficial to consider first how a law's narrative needs to be changed, and what actions best support helping others to see common ground. In other words, the law does not catalyze social change; people do.

By being clear-eyed that "the law" depends on the people behind it, and that "the law" always embodies the inherent interconnectedness between people, I think we come full circle to where we started—change often hinges on how connections within society are constructed and what efforts we need to take to rebuild, rework, or reinvigorate relationality. In turn, that reminds us that relationships involve emotional labor. We have choices to make about what feeling and framing rules we apply to a relationship, and those choices directly impact whether we move towards building connections or move away. If we better develop our capacity to unpack the ways in which feeling and framing rules are embedded into "the law," that helps us in two ways. First, we are able to make transparent for others the ways that "the law" selects certain relationships to foster and other relationships to diminish. Next, we are able to create strategies that are designed to help people build connections with each other despite the ways the law does not support those choices, and even in the face of genuine difference and disagreement.

The movement for marriage equality is an illuminating example of how activists both unpacked the law's relationality, and how activists had to choose how to navigate relational connections with other activists that at times prioritized difference and at other times prioritized unity despite difference. It will be helpful to set the stage by first reviewing how second-wave feminists in the 1960s–1970s were critiquing U.S. family law. Those feminists were highly critical of family law, and the institution of marriage more particularly, as patriarchal and as reifying the subordination of women.[9] Straight feminists mostly assumed that marriage was between a man and a woman, and did not directly take up the issue of whether that socially constructed choice, in and of itself, should be challenged. Instead, straight feminists focused their criticisms about the ways in which the law structured family relationships so that men maintained power and control and the law penalized women who acted in ways outside of the construct of a "good" wife and mother. For example, feminists objected to the ways in which family law devalued the unpaid work that a woman might undertake at home, or the ways in which family law inadequately provided for financial support for a woman and her children after a divorce.

Lesbian feminists expanded those critiques to include the ways in which the law penalized women who chose to leave a heterosexual marriage for a same-sex relation-

9. *See generally* Kate Millett, SEXUAL POLITICS: A SURPRISING EXAMINATION OF SOCIETY'S MOST ARBITRARY POLICY (1969); Shulamith Firestone, THE DIALECTIC OF SEX: THE CASE FOR FEMINIST REVOLUTION (1970); Alice Ecols, DARING TO BE BAD: RADICAL FEMINISM IN AMERICA, 1967–75 (1989).

ship—particularly the ways in which the law was used against lesbian mothers to terminate their parental rights, or was used to preclude a lesbian couple from both being recognized as parents to a child.[10] If a parent came out as a lesbian or gay, both the other straight biological parent and the state used the legal concept of the "best interests of the child" to aggressively bar the lesbian or gay parent from maintaining relationships with their children. While straight feminists and lesbian feminists each made transparent the different ways that family law privileged heterosexual men, there was not much overlap between the two groups in terms of their advocacy work. Straight feminists mostly described their work as about women's rights and equality, whereas lesbian feminists mostly described their work as about gay and lesbian rights, particularly to form family relationships that did not map onto the traditional idea of marriage.

But, in the late 1980s to early 1990s, as same-sex couples started to press for the ability to legally marry, the dynamic changed. Author and journalist Sasha Issenberg has richly detailed the dynamic unfolding of the movement for marriage equality.[11] As Issenberg notes, same-sex couples who wished to legally marry faced a legal system that unquestioningly embraced the norm that marriage was available only to a man and a woman. The idea of marriage was so resoundingly heterosexual that some courts interpreted laws that did not even specifically state that marriage was only as between a man and a woman as clearly barring marriage between same-sex couples. But, in 1993, the Hawaii State Supreme Court ruled that same-sex couples could not be denied a marriage license unless the state could show a com-

---

10. *See* Daniel Rivers, *"In the Best Interests of the Child": Lesbian and Gay Parenting Custody Cases, 1967–85*, 43 J. Soc. Hist. 917 (2010).

11. Sasha Issenberg, Engagement: America's Quarter-Century Struggle Over Same-Sex Marriage (2021).

pelling interest in that kind of discrimination.[12] While the Hawaiian Supreme Court decision did not entirely settle the question of whether same-sex marriages would be allowed, the decision was publicly received as a huge victory for "gay" marriage. The issue was framed as being about gays and lesbians having the kinds of relationships that functioned just like straight marriages, and, therefore, should be worthy of legal recognition.

Again, as Issenberg well documents, at the time of the Hawaii Supreme Court's decision, the LGBTQ community was not at all unified on the idea that its primary advocacy issue should be pursuing laws to recognize gay and lesbian marriages. Nonetheless, when the decision prompted a vigorous and hostile response from a wide range of conservative groups across the U.S., LGBTQ advocates were pressed to find common ground among themselves. If the LGBTQ community did not defend against the vitriolic attack about gay marriage, then it increased its risk of attacks along many other dimensions. Further, because conservative advocates had a multipronged attack strategy, LGBTQ advocates had to mobilize not only in the courts, but in state legislatures to defeat legislation, and on sidewalks to defeat petition-driven ballot initiatives. Advocates had to find common ground not only within the LGBTQ community, but also with straight communities—therein, the morphing of the advocacy frame from gay marriage or same-sex marriage to marriage equality. For those straight people who believed that marriage brought benefits to them and helped them flourish in their lives, then it could seem reasonable and beneficial that marriage be equally available to all. The frame became that the positive institution that is marriage benefits when all people—straight or LGBTQ—are able to marry.

---

12. *Baehr v. Lewin*, 74 Haw. 530, 852 P.2d 44 (1993).

Of course, the history of same-sex marriage is more nuanced and more complicated than presented in my very short description above. There is much more that we can learn from a more thoroughgoing study of that history.[13] But, I hope that my short version illustrates the ways in which advocates brought out family law's discriminatory relationality and asserted the injustices that such discrimination caused. Then, we see how advocates had to make a range of choices about where and how to build common ground in order to bring together enough people to build power to change the law. Those choices included some activists agreeing to get behind the effort for marriage equality even while they remained skeptical of marriage itself. Similarly, other groups, particularly straight allies, had to forthrightly face their own biases about LGBTQ communities, and to learn how to be an ally without washing over valuable differences. Nonetheless, in foundational ways, people working towards marriage equality made choices to foreground interconnectedness, not adversarial relationality. Of course, relationality within the broadest version of the movement was dynamic—as human relationality always is. There were fissures, fluid alliances, and challenges with hyper-loyalty. There also were enough people committed strongly enough to cultivating common ground to keep the movement on track. Further, even though marriage equality is the law, movement dynamism continues. There continue to be legal and legislative challenges that put marriage equality at risk, and there continue to be community members and activists who do not view marriage as a just institution and press for further social change.

I hope that my examples about the law and its relationality convincingly demonstrate how "the law" is not removed from

---

13. *See* Lillian Faderman, THE GAY REVOLUTION: THE STORY OF THE STRUGGLE (2015); William Eskridge & Christopher Riano, MARRIAGE EQUALITY: FROM OUTLAWS TO IN-LAWS (2020).

the people who make it or the people upon whom it is applied. I hope my examples also show how the law includes, and tries to orchestrate, emotional labor. The emotional labor embedded in a law—its feeling and framing rules—are a critical mechanism used to try and ensure that people follow the law in a particular way. Finally, I hope my examples help reveal how investigating law's relationality provides important information to activists—information about a law's justness or unjustness, information about how the people who made the law are trying to maintain power and control, and information about how activists might reframe the law so as to find a way to better build a coalition to change the law. Activists need to be aware of all of those features of the law in order to craft the best set of strategies for social change.

Conclusion

As activists, we often hear the refrain "keep your eyes on the prize." The phrase suggests that we would be better at bringing about social change if we concentrated on our desired end goals instead of getting caught up in the rough and tumble of our everyday experiences in social movement work. I think the phrase also implies that part of the rough and tumble that can derail an activist are the emotions and emotional labor involved in activist work. As we have examined one of the central emotions of activism—anger—we have seen some ways in which it can distract and disrupt. We also have considered some important justifications for anger, and its aptness at signaling dignitary harms. Critically, I hope it has become clear that activists often learn specific feeling and framing rules related to anger, like hyper-loyalty, and specific actions, like public protest, which can cause us to move too quickly and too easily into anger that is caustic and retributive. That then hampers us from creating the conditions needed to produce our desired social change.

The corrective already is imbedded in a core feature of emotions—that emotions are an endeavor involving a web of relationships. We experience emotions largely because we interact with others around us. We experience both our own embodied sensations that we label as an emotion as well as interpret cues from others to assess the emotions we think they are sensing. We need to remind ourselves that every web of relationships is dynamic. That includes dynamism about how we envision who is within (or outside of) a web of relationships, and also what kinds of emotions are present, absent, or changing within that web. I have suggested that activists overcommit to bright or firm relational lines, and that our relational habits and actions are hard to disrupt. We are quick to see "us" and "them," and to assume harmony inside our group and adversarialness outside of our group. Because of those habits, I encouraged us to consider a different path—the interior path, or the path of quiet, open-inquiring contemplation. Taking lessons from several faith traditions, I demonstrated that we can learn reflective practices that open us to unexpected connections and unexpected ways to make progress in our social change work.

Ultimately, I have tried to build confidence in the idea of radical relationality—a kind of relationality that is acutely aware of histories of subordination as well as histories of flourishing. Radical relationality builds on the commitments of mutual aid, and enhances our ability to build connections alongside differences and disagreements. It allows us to build towards social change, not fracture ourselves into micromovements.

Finally, when we apply radical relationality to the law, it helps us see how those in power use the law to maintain power. We can see beyond individual, adversarial disputes to the underlying system that is designed to control and divide. That then helps illuminate common ground that has been hidden, and can provide us with opportunities to build the fulsome support that is needed to effectively change entrenched systems. Radical relationality is not a panacea and does not happen without effort, success, and failure. I hope, however, that radical relationality offers us a new frame to use as we approach the hard work of social change, and provides us a set of habits that build connections, not barriers.

Index